THE
FUTURE WORLD
OF
TRANSPORTATION

Walt Disney World.
EPCOT Center Book

THE
FUTURE WORLD
OF
TRANSPORTATION

By Valerie Moolman
and the Editors of Grolier

GROLIER

Grolier Incorporated
President and Chairman of the Board Robert B. Clarke

STAFF FOR THIS BOOK
Editor in Chief Kenneth W. Leish
Senior Editor Bernard M. Garfinkel
Art Director Don Longabucco
Picture Editors Laurie Platt Winfrey
Diane Raines Ward
Editorial Assistant Susan Stellingwerf
Production Manager Valerie Plue
Assistant Production Manager Margaret Fina
Consultant Daniel Roos, Director, Center for
Transportation Studies, Massachusetts
Institute of Technology

COVER: "Lift-off! We have lift-off!" Space Shuttle Challenger soars into space on June 18, 1983—a spectacular sight that never fails to thrill viewers.

TITLE PAGE: Propelled by a nitrogen-powered backpack called the Manned Maneuvering Unit (MMU), Astronaut Bruce McCandless II flies through space in February 1984.

Library of Congress Cataloging in Publication Data

Moolman, Valerie.
 The future world of transportation.

 Summary: Traces the history and discusses the future of transportation with emphasis on the development of different types of vehicles and modes of transport. Based on the "World of Motion" exhibit at Walt Disney's EPCOT Center.

 1. Transportation—Juvenile literature. [1. Transportation] I. Title.
TA1149.M66 1984 629.04 84-10787
ISBN 0-7172-8141-8

ACKNOWLEDGMENTS
The author and the editors gratefully acknowledge the assistance of the following: Harry A. Turton, Resident Manager, World of Motion, General Motors Corporation; William M. Spreitzer, Head of Transportation Research Department, General Motors Research Laboratories, Warren, Michigan; Jesco von Puttkamer and Burton Edelson, NASA; James A. Arey, Pan American Airways; Lloyd Money, U.S. Department of Transportation; James Costantino, Director of Transportation Systems Center, U.S. Department of Transportation; Janice W. Bain, Transportation Research Board, National Research Council, National Academy of Science; Willis M. Hawkins, Senior Advisor, Lockheed Corporation; and Wilfred Owen, Guest Scholar, the Brookings Institution.

PICTURE CREDITS
The picture editors would like to express particular appreciation to Michael Melford and Wheeler Pictures for creative photography at EPCOT Center; NASA; the American Heritage Library; and Cooper/West/Nicholas Enterprises of London, who provided the artwork that appears on pages 8–9, 52, 56–57, 58–59, 74–75, 78–79, 80–81, 90–91, 96–97, and 109. The illustrators include Tom Stimpson, Lionel Jeans, Andy Farmer, Mike Saunders, Chris Forsey, and Geoff Taylor. Pages 3,6: NASA 10,11: General Motors 13: Goodyear 14–21, 24–25: Michael Melford 22: General Motors 26: Brown Brothers 28: Art Resource (2) 31: top, Radio Times Hulton; bottom, Library of Congress 33: New York Central Rail Road (3) 34: bottom, Collection Georges Sirot 35: David Phillips Collection 36: top, General Motors; bottom, Culver 37: top left, Lester Levy Collection, Johns Hopkins University; top right, Academic American Encyclopedia; bottom, Culver 38: Courtesy Mitchell Beazley, Ltd. and Random House, Inc. 40: top, Museum of the City of New York; bottom, New-York Historical Society 41: top, Marine Historical Society; bottom, Cunard Archives 42: bottom, Prado/Newsweek Books 44: Library of Congress (2) 46: top, Musée de l'Air, Paris; center, University of Washington; bottom, Douglas Aircraft 47: top left, Eastern Airlines; left center, Wide World; left bottom, Radio Times Hulton; right bottom, Bell Aerospace 48: David Schleinkofer 50: Robert Azzi/Woodfin Camp 51: George Hall/Woodfin Camp 54: Touring Club of France 55: center, Seth Joel/Wheeler Pictures; bottom, Early Winters 61: top, General Motors; bottom, Transit Post 62: Culver 63: Dennis Brack/Black Star 64: top, John Dominis/Wheeler Pictures; bottom, American High Speed Rail 66: Photo Researchers Inc. 68: John McGrail/Wheeler Pictures 69–70: Academic American Encyclopedia 72: top, General Motors, bottom, NASA 73: General Motors 77: bottom, Michael Melford/Wheeler Pictures 83 and 85, left: Pan American Airways 84,85 top: Academic American Encyclopedia 85 bottom: Mitchell Beazley/Random House 86: top, Jean Guichard/Sygma; bottom, Alain DeJean/Sygma 87: Anthony Wolfe/Rainbow 88: NASA (3) 89: left, General Motors; right, Grumman 92: Anthony Wolfe/Rainbow 95: Williams International Affairs 98: Smithsonian Institution 99–107: NASA

Contents

Four suffragettes in a shiny Model-T Ford, circa 1917.

CHAPTER 1

Report from the Year 2050

It is mid-morning on a steamy day in August 2050. A big transport plane is waiting to be loaded at the Catskill Air Terminal, 150 miles from New York City. But it is not standing on the runway. Instead, the huge airliner is hovering over the terminal, five hundred feet in the air, like an oversize blimp.

Flight 8679, departing the New York City area for the West Coast and Australia, is not a blimp. It is the newest kind of passenger airliner, an Ultra Jet *(see Glossary)*. Twice the size of the historic 747, it travels at a speed of close to three thousand miles an hour—three times the speed of early supersonic transports.

Like many transcontinental planes in the year 2050, it is a double-decker. It carries passengers on its main deck and a load of autoplanes *(see Glossary)* in its ferry-car compartment. In spite of its huge size, it is as graceful as a bird in flight, with a gently curving body and thin wings.

Still hovering in the air, the plane begins to load. Some passengers prefer to fly their own personal autoplanes directly into the Ultra Jet from the departure gates at the terminal. These autoplanes are stored in the ferry-car compartment until passengers arrive at their destination. Then they fly off the Ultra Jet one by one as the giant ship opens its ramp doors while hovering in the air over the airport.

Passengers who prefer to use the air-taxi service are also boarding the Ultra Jet now. These passengers are unloaded from tiny auto-aircabs that shuttle up into the sky from the terminal to the plane like bees entering a hive. The auto-aircabs lock onto the side of the Ultra Jet as passengers step into the plane through a special air-pressure door. At their destination, these passengers will leave the plane in the same way.

At any time at any of the world's major airports, several of these big Ultras are in the sky, loading for takeoff. Their cargo doors are open like land-

A bold plan for a Space Operations Center, designed by the Boeing Aerospace Company for NASA. The shuttle orbiter, lower left, would serve as a construction base for the permanently manned spaceport, which would function as a staging point for other space operations.

7

ing ramps to receive or discharge tiny auto shuttles and baggage cars. More conventional planes, which offer around-the-clock service to points within several hundred miles, are loading at the terminal. They are parked around the circular terminal building. Their passengers board them at departure gates, which they reach by elevator from the terminal's lower levels. Airports in the old days had terminals and loading gates scattered over a

wide area. This airport of 2050 is almost all underground—except for its long runways, which are constructed of a special plastic that absorbs the noise of takeoff.

In 2050 it is much easier to get to airports than in the past. Visitors can use the fly-your-car service or various systems of autocars that link towns and terminal via computerized superhighways. Long air trips are easier to make, and cheaper. The South Sea Islands and the Great Barrier Reef are only a few hours away for vacationers around the world.

There is still only one terminal for space flight, the Earth International Space Port near Tucson, Arizona. It is used largely by people who have business on the satellite space stations, or "spacehabs," or by those going to one of the new space

A parade of auto shuttles flies passengers and baggage up to a huge Ultra Jet in this depiction of a busy international airport in the year 2050. The circular terminal tower, topped by a domed observation deck, is shown at left.

station resorts. There are very few of these resorts, which keeps them out of reach of all but the extremely rich. But prices may soon be coming down. The business pages of the *New York–Boston Times* are now full of stories about the struggle between two great international hotel-and-travel chains to capture the vacation market in space.

On a more practical level, in the decades since 2000 the Federal Aviation Agency and other air control agencies throughout the world have completely modernized the air traffic control system. At first, this was done to take care of the growing volume of traffic in the 1980s and 1990s. More recently, the system was modernized again to allow it to handle new types of air traffic. A worldwide network of controllers now uses advanced computers to program flights for all craft from origin to destination. The computers guide the flights through carefully selected paths of air space down to their final approach.

Back in the cockpit of flight 8671, the captain and the copilot watch their instrument panels as the onboard computer completes the takeoff checklist. The computer then closes the cargo doors and turns on the recorded safety instructions that used to be spoken by the flight attendants. Flight attendants are still considered an essential part of airline service. There was a move in about 2010 to replace them with robots. But the labor unions and the flying public protested. Now planes carry an even greater number of flight attendants with specialties ranging from stenography to medical assistance.

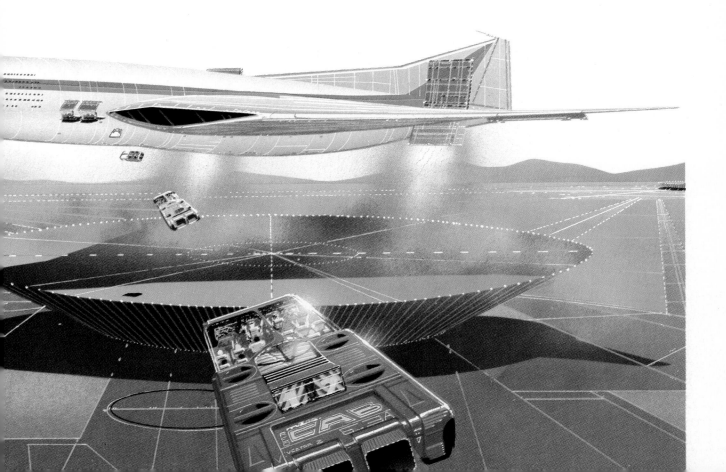

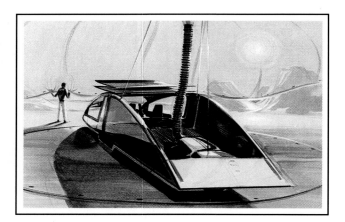

This camper of the future carries its own plastic vacation house, which can be inflated anywhere.

Like a huge fish, this pressurized, two-passenger sport submersible explores the ocean depths.

The Ultra Jet rises as quietly as if it were a lighter-than-air machine, climbing higher and higher, almost straight up into the sky. Then the plane's flight pattern changes. The flight deck computer transfers power to the directional jets. The huge plane angles higher to cruising altitude and speed. But in the cabin, passengers feel no sensation of speed. The Ultra Jet is now so far above the ground that it is nearly invisible and soundless from below. From its decks, even on a clear day, the earth is little more than a blur.

Cruising in Comfort

Some travelers are not in a hurry and regard the view from above as one of the thrills of a pleasure trip. For these people, a dirigible flight is an even better way to fly. There was some concern about the return of these great airships due to their early history of disaster. But careful testing has shown that the twenty-first-century models are as nearly accidentproof as any vehicle on the move today. They use nonflammable gas and materials. They have sturdy yet flexible structures. They fly with computerized flight programming and guidance systems. And their air and ground crews receive expert training. All these and other fail-safe factors combine to ensure the safety of dirigible travel. There is nothing to beat one of these skyliners for a comfortable round-the-world cruise.

Looking down from an airship's observation deck to the lands and seas below, we see a world that is a fascinating panorama of change. It is a study in contrasts between the old and the startlingly new. There are great cities whose centers date back to the fifteenth century and whose outskirts soar high with the graceful towers of the twenty-first. Other cities that were dazzlingly modern a hundred years ago are now beginning to look their age. Their newest features are recently built rooftop heliports and numerous great highways that circle around them like threads around a spool. Change occurs even faster in some of the older communities of Europe and the even more ancient ones of the Orient. In these cities, new transportation systems seem to be put into place almost daily. Sometimes this produces the extreme contrast of animal-drawn carts traveling on dirt tracks that run beneath an eight-lane elevated highway.

Similar examples of change may be observed in the developing countries. Old-fashioned bicycles and ancient gas-guzzling automobiles are still used as means of personal transportation in many developing countries. But the adoption of new technologies has also enabled some of these nations to emerge, almost overnight, among the world's leaders in well-planned railways, highway systems, and other transportation facilities.

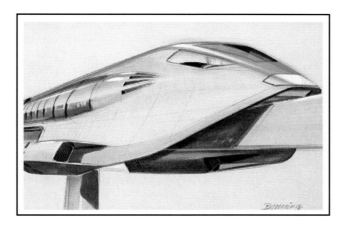

The Maglev train, seen at EPCOT Center's World of Motion, rides friction-free on magnetic waves.

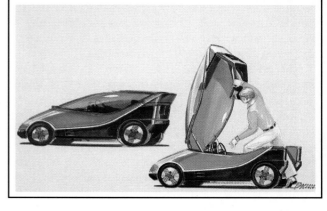

A two-rider subcompact car with a full-length canopy that would simplify construction and keep costs low.

Still, old-timers can take heart at what's happening downtown in America and Europe. More and more mid-city areas have been completely closed to the traffic that used to clog them. Visitors to those areas leave their autos in a parking tower or exit from the short-run rapid transit system. Then they complete their trips to the shopping and business centers in small, automated electric vehicles or on moving walkways. Both of these systems were introduced to the world at least a century ago. But they were not developed for large-scale public use until the second decade of the twenty-first century.

It was thought for a time that the automobile as it was known throughout the twentieth century would be seen only in museums by now. True, some of the great cars of the past—such as the Model-T Ford, Daimler, Stutz-Bearcat, Pierce-Arrow, Cadillac, Ferrari, and Corvette—are museum pieces. But they are objects of admiration and affection rather than a curiosity. They are the ancestors of the cars of today. We are still an automobile society and will continue to be so as long as human beings regard the car as a symbol of independence and the best means of personal transportation.

Autos on the roads today are of various types, some more automatic than others. Many are the extremely durable, driver-operated gasoline-en-gine cars of the 2030s and 2040s. Others are the sleek little one- and two-person electric runabouts first designed back in the 1990s. A growing number of the current crop, however, are larger and carry more passengers than those seen in the past. They are more fully automated so that the driver's duties are reduced to a minimum and safety is a built-in factor.

In automobile transportation, there is a clear and continuing trend toward safety and computer control. Cars are built for special purposes, such as long- or short-distance travel. Computerized traffic controls regulate traffic flow. Anticollision systems have nearly made accidents a thing of the past.

Much more change is evident in railroads, at least in some areas of the world. In the United States, the railroad system is still used mainly for shipping freight. There is high-speed passenger service within major clusters of cities, such as New York–Washington–Boston. But for long-distance travel, people prefer to go by air.

In other countries, however, the development of rocket trains and other new kinds of power systems have led to greatly increased use of the railroad for all but long-distance journeys. Fast and efficient rail systems in Japan, France, Germany, England, Switzerland, Canada, and some sectors of the Middle East, Africa, and Latin America now reduce what were daylong journeys to a couple of hours. Already well under way are expansions of these lines, which will link country with country and even continent with continent.

For short-distance runs, such as commuter trips, varieties of PeopleMovers are in place throughout the world *(see Glossary)*. Some run on old-fashioned standard tracks, and some need no tracks at all. Some run underground or are otherwise concealed in tubes, while others run on overhead guideways. Once seen only at airports and exhibition parks, they are now everywhere.

Now, as our giant airship dips down over the countryside and the sea, it is likely to pass many other lighter-than-air ships. But the majority of them are not used primarily to carry people. When the lighter-than-air craft began to make their gradual comeback in the late 1980s, they were used for cargo more often than for passengers because of their great weight-lifting capacity and leisurely pace. Now that they have increased their speed somewhat and improved their passenger facilities, they have become a popular way for people to travel. Yet they are still the workhorses of the sky. At construction sites, air terminals, and docksides, we can see powerful freight blimps and dirigibles hoisting enormous loads or lowering them into container ships. All of this is done at the direction of robots. But today's automatons are not the lovable tin men of the early sci-fi space adventures. Rather, they are sleek machines, all joints and angles, with a workman's personality all their own.

Under the Sea and to the Stars

The bustling seaports of the old world have also taken on a different look. Dealing with huge cargoes of freight from inland waterways and highways, they are clean and modern. They suggest high efficiency rather than adventure and romance. Yet something seems to stir. New things will soon be happening. As we shall see, different kinds of great ships will challenge the ocean in different ways. Until then, many people continue to long for the good old days of the luxury ocean liner. A fortunate few still take glorious vacation trips on ocean liners. But the elegant seagoing giants are very nearly extinct as a species. For short trips on sea or lake or river, most people take fast-moving hovercraft, which skim across the water like low-flying birds *(see Glossary)*.

Under water is where the action is. Scientists are now beginning to tame the depths of the seas. Looking down from the dirigible's observation deck, we may catch sight of one of the first of what promises to be a great many floating cities, and perhaps also see the tops of some submerged ones. Both kinds are based on the deep-sea drilling platforms and submarines and aircraft carriers of yesterday. The possibilities for extensive underwater farming and living are being explored on an experimental basis in several seas. Those who venture beneath the waves can see new types of submarine vehicles working the waters between and around the undersea stations. It is these high-powered subboats that suggest an exciting future for longer-distance underwater shipping. The sea frontier, almost ignored for so many years, is at last being investigated—long after the sky pioneers have made their homes in space.

After dark we may see the lights of one of the larger space stations. High above us are space workshops, space farms, space laboratories, space colonies, and space playgrounds. All of them confirm the predictions made by our more optimistic scientists three-quarters of a century ago. At the Tucson Earth International Space Port, there are daily rocket flights into space. And several nations operate their own earth ports to connect with their space habitats and to launch new probes of the stars. Shuttles from earth to the Upper Port far out in space are regular but infrequent. The cost of the energy needed for these long flights is very high.

We still look up into space with a sense of awe as we realize that we know people up there, and that other pioneers will soon be exploring even farther into outer space. It all happened so swiftly, once it began, and yet . . . the true beginning was a very long time ago.

This helium-filled blimp, conceived by Goodyear, would be 400 feet long and could carry loads, such as the bridge section shown here, of up to 40 tons.

CHAPTER 2

Exploring World of Motion at EPCOT Center

Throughout history, there has scarcely been a time when man has not dreamed and been laughed at for dreaming. Whoever first thought of floating downstream on a log or climbing on the back of an animal to take the weight off his own feet surely attracted laughter and jeers. And as for someone trying to dream up some kind of machine that would go farther and faster—why, that was obviously ridiculous.

But when an idea worked, those who doubted became silent . . . until the next wild-eyed dreamer tried to make life easier. A horseless carriage? Whatever for? You want to fly? You must be crazy.

For centuries, dreamers were laughed at for trying to fly with homemade wings or for building a human-powered flying machine. But why shouldn't man be capable of discovering the secret of flight? It was obvious that birds do it, bees do it, even airborne autumn leaves do it. Why shouldn't we do it?

We wouldn't have discovered the secret of flight if everybody had thought it was impossible. Certainly it was difficult. Great mental energy, imagination, and determination were needed to overcome personal problems, lack of money, and the doubts of so-called experts.

In 1901, Rear Admiral George W. Melville, Chief Engineer of the United States Navy, gave a speech in which he said: "If God had intended that man should fly he would have given him wings. . . . The airship business is a fake and has been so since it was started 200 years ago. . . . Never has the human mind so persistently evaded the issue,

---

A sleek, 250-passenger elevated monorail carries visitors to Walt Disney World past the General Motors Corporation's World of Motion at EPCOT Center.

Deceptively compact, the wheel-shaped World of Motion (above) is 65 feet high and 320 feet in diameter. Guests board chaircars (below) that take them on a tour of transportation's past and future.

begged the question, and, wrangling resolutely with the facts, insisted upon dreams being accepted as actual performance.''

Two years later, the Wright brothers of Dayton, Ohio, achieved powered, controlled flight in a heavier-than-air vehicle over the sandy beach of North Carolina's Outer Banks.

Wilbur and Orville Wright had dared to dream, and had then turned their dream into actual performance. Having wrangled ''resolutely with the facts,'' they established new aeronautic principles and achieved what most of the world had thought impossible.

Human beings do that all the time—but only those who have an optimistic view of the future and dare to make imaginative leaps.

At EPCOT Center in Walt Disney World there is a striking structure of shining stainless steel. Sixty-five feet high and 320 feet in diameter, this mas-

sive wheel-shaped building is the General Motors "World of Motion" exhibit. More than any other symbol, the wheel stands for human progress through transportation: wheels roll, people move, a need is filled, a trail is blazed, one destination is reached, and another goal is set.

World of Motion consists of two hemispheres, one containing an entertaining yet informative review of the past, the other presenting a more serious yet exciting look into the future. Visitors to the first hemisphere board a train of audio-equipped chaircars and take a leisurely 14.5-minute ride over a quarter-mile course, during which they marvel at twenty-four ingeniously animated scenes. These miniplays, featuring 140 life-size and lifelike human and animal figures, offer a lighthearted look at the history of transportation.

Every hour, up to thirty-two hundred passengers ride in the six-seater open cars. They are treated to a celebration of the quest for mobility, an exploration of mankind's continuing attempt to solve the problems of moving from one place to another. The exhibit is a collection of comic scenes reflecting serious matters. There are cave people soothing their aching feet. There are bold adventurers braving primitive waterways in dugout, raft, or simple sailboat. There are hopeful travelers, merchants for the most part, trying to persuade a variety of stubborn animals to submit to being beasts of burden. Ultimately, some animals did, but only after mankind had gone on foot for thousands of years.

A man's limit for a day's foot travel was about fifteen to twenty miles, and the most he could carry for much of that time was a burden of some ninety pounds. Then, about seven thousand years ago, man trained an ox or an ass to transport his pack. He found that the beast could carry more than three times the amount a human being could load onto his own shoulders. Next it occurred to him to place even larger burdens onto a land sledge of sorts. This was little more than a platform set on crude wooden runners. The sledge was hitched to a pair of oxen. By this means, he could transport a load of some three thousand pounds—but slowly, and at much discomfort to the oxen.

The World of Motion chaircar rounds a bend and a great breakthrough bursts upon the scene: the replacement of wooden runners by the wheel. In a Middle Eastern throne room, several hopeful inventors are offering their versions of a device intended to make sledges go more smoothly and much faster. A square shape is rejected, and a triangular one too. The triangle is interesting, but not quite what is needed, and its inventor looks disappointed. Little does he know that thousands of years later an organization called NASA will develop a vehicle with triangular wheels for traveling on rugged cliffsides or over deep cracks and crevices. But it is of course the round wheel that is the smash hit in this scene from long ago.

The actual inventor of the wheel remains unknown. But we do know that some time in the fourth millennium B.C., in the fertile crescent of the Tigris and Euphrates rivers, some warrior or farmer or traveler or sledgemaker achieved an incredible technological leap forward in the shape of the wheel. In its first known form, seen in a sketch made in Sumer about 3500 B.C., it appears on a boxy vehicle equipped with a sledgelike undercarriage . . . and two pairs of wheels.

With those first wheels, a system of land transportation was born. And the wheel was gradually refined with time. It became more smoothly rounded, and was set on sturdy axles supporting a stoutly built wagon. In that form, the wheel made it possible for a yoke of oxen to pull a load at least two or three times heavier than before. The beginnings of a stream of traffic carrying goods and people from one place to another made tracks, then paths, then rough highways for other vehicles to follow.

Yet the oxcart was slow. Wheels or no wheels, its animal power could manage scarcely more than a mile and a half per hour. How to make the vehicle go faster? Get a horse! Get more horses. Get better horses. Streamline that horse-drawn wagon into a chariot or carriage. Get a better engine than a horse. Build a better road. Run a steam-powered machine on a roadbed of steel. Pave over the dirt tracks and put rubber on the wheels and the horsepower under a hood and yourself into the driver's seat . . . .

Looking back through time, riders of World of Motion chaircars catch glimpses of the early days of steam, of flight, of America's love affair with the automobile. Then the action quickens. There is a sense of riding in an automobile of the 1960s and speeding up to the seventies and eighties. The final ride begins with a zoom down a tree-lined highway, which miraculously captures the sheer joy of living in motion. As the scenery flashes by, we sense ourselves leaving the road and our vehicle becoming something else. Is it a snowmobile? A bobsled? A speedboat? A low-flying aircraft? Whatever it is, it races between snowbanks, cuts through wavetops, flies low over farmlands, and then rises as the land suddenly falls away beneath us. Higher and higher we soar, at what appears to be a dizzying speed. (In fact the autocar is moving at a rate of two feet per second; it is the filmed scenery that gives the impression of terrific speed.)

We are in a jet, flying even higher and faster, until we leave earth's atmosphere and become the occupants of a spaceship floating over a city in deep space. Judging by the flow of traffic around us, this city serves as an extraterrestrial transit terminal. The space is actually CenterCore, the sixty-foot-high core of the exhibit building, but it seems to stretch on forever.

After a pause to view the awe-inspiring sight of tomorrow's community being served by tomorrow's transportation system, we bank gracefully around it and descend lightly to earth . . . landing in a craft that again becomes the chaircar we started in. But now there is a difference: as we look at ourselves in the mirrored tunnel toward the end

In World of Motion, the progress of transportation is depicted in a series of amusing scenes, such as the one below of a train robbery during the age of steam.

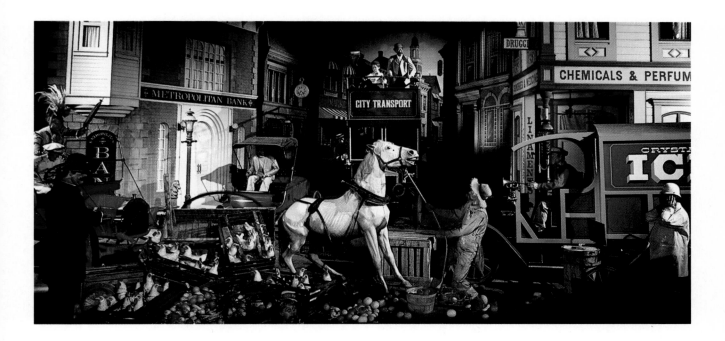

of the ride, we appear to be not in the little open cars we boarded but in elegantly streamlined, transparent bubble cars of the twenty-first century.

The ride ends in the main exhibit area. It's been more than a joyride. We have seen how the development of transportation systems has speeded up the evolution of society. We have seen how the spread of civilization has followed the opening of a trail by early pathfinders; the crossing of an ocean by seafarers in flimsy boats; the linking of coasts by railroad tracks and puffing steam engines. And at the end of the ride, we have learned how each step has led to yet another step and ultimately to a world of tomorrow that is on the horizon.

The second hemisphere of World of Motion is the ground-floor Transcenter, a 33,000-square-foot walk-through exhibit area that demonstrates how close we already are to a future dreamed up long ago by science-fiction writers.

Each display offers a look at an early tomorrow and poses fascinating questions.

Will motorists of the near future have a choice between the following: a superstreamlined four-seater that gets seventy-one miles to the gallon or

The appearance of the automobile on Main Street U.S.A. marked a great advance in transportation, but scenes of total confusion (above) were not uncommon.

Barnstorming pilots, like the one shown below with an admirer, were glamorous figures in the 1920s.

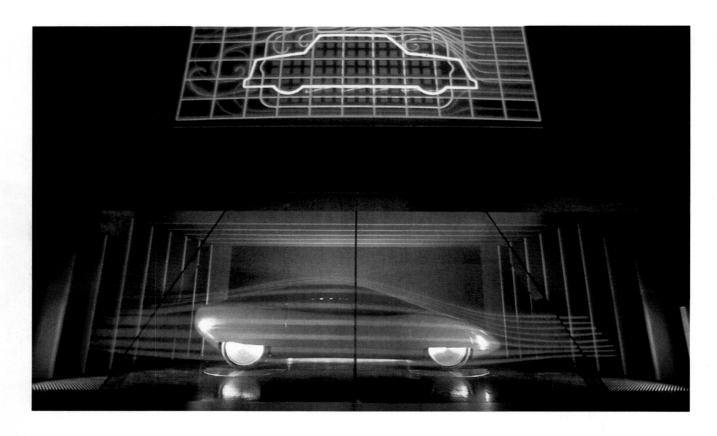

The Aerotest display shows how wind tunnel tests improve automotive design. The goal is to reduce drag and increase fuel efficiency. Cars use up to 65 percent of their fuel to push through the air.

a three-wheel minicar for commuters that almost triples that fuel mileage or a tiny auto that uses no gasoline at all but instead turns sunlight into motor-driving electricity?

Can the commuters of today look forward to a tomorrow in which they will be rushed downtown in trains that float along smoothly and silently, supported not by wheels but by magnetic energy and powered by electric current?

Are there other automotive power plants on the horizon? A coal-fired turbine engine, perhaps *(see Glossary, Turbine Engine)?* Or one that runs on hydrogen removed from water? Mixed units that might combine a flywheel and a turbine or a turbine and an electric motor?

Will vacationers someday be able to take a low-flying cruise in a hovercraft hotel? One that simultaneously provides shelter, travel, refreshment, and recreation as it skims over land and sea?

Or will they have the option of driving their recreation vehicles through wilderness areas, finding themselves a campsite, and then inflating a vacation home stored in the rear of their vehicle?

These questions are based on reality, not fantasy. Designs, models, and in some cases working models already exist. A few are being used in the workaday world. The others—and many more—can be seen at "Dreamers Workshop"—ideas that have been pursued through designs, models, tests, and more tests. The exhibit's theme is the concept of an idea being born, taking shape, developing, and changing. Not surprisingly, most of the ideas illustrated here have to do with the automobile. The shapes of various imagined vehicles are projected one after another onto a screen

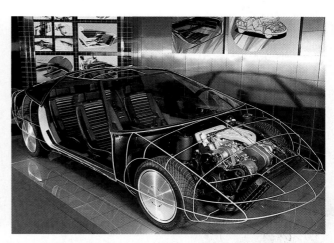

The experimental Aero 2000, a four-passenger subcompact exhibited in World of Motion, was developed with the aid of computers. It has many features that make it aerodynamically efficient. The TV screens on the dashboard provide a rear view and a map of the driver's route.

Developed by General Motors, the 350-pound Lean Machine is a three-wheeled, one-passenger vehicle that combines the characteristics of a car and a motorcycle. It is agile, stable, and fuel efficient.

that looks like a profile of a human head. The practical dreamer dreams before taking up work tools.

Is it a little fanciful for a major manufacturing company to play so strongly on the theme of dreams as an essential step toward achievement? Not when the spirit of Charles F. Kettering is present throughout Dreamers Workshop. "Boss Ket," as he was known, was not a fanciful man, even though he was a dreamer. He became head of General Motors Research Corporation at the end of World War I and remained the company's guiding inventor-genius for twenty-seven years. He welcomed challenges and the opportunities to effect change. "The opportunities of man are only limited by his imagination," he would say. "Do something different! My God! Do something different!"

From Idea to Reality

First comes the need. Then comes the inspiration and the pushing around of parts of ideas in the mind. A mental design begins to form. Now for the drawing board. On one side are the familiar sketch pads, pencils, paints, and brushes; on the other, an electronic screen that is part of a CAD, or a Computer-Aided-Design device.

The idea takes shape in a series of designs, each more detailed than the one before. Each element and each combination of elements is fed into a computer as the concept approaches concrete form. The process is more than an aid to design: long before the vehicle reaches the test track, its various parts and their combinations are pretested by computer.

One of the creations to emerge from this process is an automobile called the Aero 2000.

A two-door four-seater, the Aero 2000 represents a breakthrough in automotive design. It is a frontwheel-drive subcompact powered by an experimental three-cylinder, turbo-charged 68-h.p. diesel engine, and it is as fuel-efficient as General Motors' best current frontwheel-drive subcompact. What is at present just a model developed for the exhibit could, if built, achieve seventy-one miles to the gallon, thanks not only to its engine but to its aerodynamic design. The surface is sleek: nothing sticks out that will cause wind resistance. The front wheels are curtained by skirts or shields that open only when a turn exceeds ten degrees. The underside of the body is enclosed. The window glass is unframed, flush with the body and bonded to it. Handles have been eliminated from the sliding doors . . . .

No handles? The doors, and not only the doors, are voice-activated. The Aero 2000's computer operates space-age devices that can see, hear, speak, and respond to voice commands. The computer provides not only driver and passenger convenience but a way to control the vehicle as well. We've seen it in the movies and on television; now we see it in real life. And there is more: radar-activated brakes; an instrument panel display that pinpoints the vehicle's position on a computerized or telecast map; and an entertainment-communications system, which includes a telephone and a radio that can be linked to a satellite. The Aero 2000 symbolizes a new era in personal transportation—a stylish, superstreamlined four-seater that sets new standards in operating efficiency, gas mileage, and passenger comfort and convenience.

The Aero 2000 revolves silently on a turntable near another revolutionary new motor vehicle called the Lean Machine.

In fact, at first glance this object looks like a well-fed bug, although to some observers it resembles a rocket. A second glance shows that it has three wheels and suggests that it might be some kind of training motorcycle. A third reveals the vehicle as an automobile. For an automobile, it is lean. And short. And low-slung. And light. Three feet wide, ten feet two inches long, four feet high to the top of its canopy, and weighing only four hundred pounds. Sleek.

And it does actually lean. Or rather, it tilts.

The Lean Machine was inspired by the commuter traffic in and around such clogged major cities as Detroit and New York. Countless thousands of passenger vehicles cram the business routes during rush hour. Most of them are four-passenger cars transporting a single individual. It's as if nobody ever heard about car-pooling. Some brave souls challenge traffic on their bicycles. A noisy few ride motorcycles. Whatever their other virtues or defects, at least these two-wheelers don't waste space and gas by carrying empty seats.

From this example comes an idea! Surely what is needed is a small, sub-subcompact, single-passenger, all-weather vehicle. With maybe an extra seat for a second passenger?

Photovoltaic cells in the roof of an experimental two-seater (above) turn sunlight into electricity to help power the electric motor. To the left in the photo is a car with a coal-fired gas turbine engine.

Thus, the Lean Machine. Similar to a motorcycle in size and weight, it is essentially a one-person vehicle that can accelerate to sixty miles per hour in seven seconds and travel up to two hundred miles on a gallon of gas. Like motorcyclists, drivers of the Lean Machine can preserve their balance as they lean into turns by using the vehicle's pedal-operated tilting capacity.

But there the comparison with the motorcycle ends. The Lean Machine rests firmly on its own three wheels, one in front and two in the rear. It encloses and protects its driver in a fiberglass passenger compartment with a clear plastic canopy. The passenger compartment contains an automobile control center in miniature. Steering, braking, and throttle controls are combined in the handlebars. Automatic transmission is linked to a rear-mounted, liquid-cooled, 38-h.p. engine housed in a lower unit.

When the Lean Machine takes curves in the manner of a motorcycle, the upper and lower units operate independently. The passenger compartment rotates horizontally and separately from the lower unit. By controlling this rotation a driver can lean into turns while the lower unit stays upright.

As for air resistance, it is less than one-fifth that of a motorcycle and one-eighth that of an automobile. There is virtually nothing about the Lean Machine's shape to interfere with its low gas consumption.

Visions of the Future

A car that talks back to its owner, a three-wheel commuter autocycle with a rotating passenger compartment . . . Gimmicks? Hardly. They're not on the roads yet, but they very soon could be in similar if not exactly the same form.

These ultramodern but very real vehicles are typical of the ideas Dreamers Workshop presents in a gallery filled with designs and models for new vehicles and transport systems. All are out of the ordinary, but some are already beginning to be used in various parts of the world. They have been created by individuals who have let their imaginations leap over the boundaries of the commonplace. Designed for land and sea and air, they have the streamlined, clean look of the future without appearing in any way fantastic. The thought that leaps to mind on seeing them is not, "What crazy kind of gizmo is that?" but, "Why don't we already have it?"

Why don't we? The list of reasons begins with their cost-effectiveness and continues from there. But there is no such reason as, "It's a fool idea and it'll never work." Whatever "it" is, it will work in some form or another. Probably only a few of these ideas will ever be built exactly as shown because technologies and public needs continue to change. But all these visions of the future, imaginative though they may be, have been designed by practical dreamers for practical purposes.

There are many more models hanging from the ceiling of the workshop, displayed in showcases, stacked on shelves and racks, sitting on scale-model tracks and roadways, floating on imaginary seas, and suspended in space. They are all the dreamer's dreams of today and the promises of tomorrow. Cars that can be driven or flown. Monorails—trains that ride a single rail on an elevated roadway. Magnetically levitated trains that float above tracks within an air space created by magnets *(see Glossary)*. Giant helicopters and super-

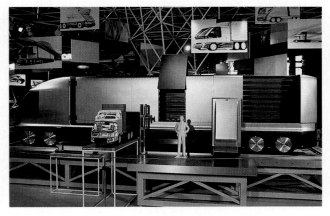

On display in World of Motion are models of the Aero Freighter (above), a futuristic, fuel-efficient container truck, and the Transeat (top), a vehicle for the elderly; special wheels assure a smooth ride.

The Wilderbus (above) is an off-road touring bus with articulated wheels that can accommodate 50 passengers. The Maglev high-speed train at top is lifted and propelled by electromagnets.

size airships with two cigar-shaped hulls to haul huge loads through the air. Sleek, large cross-country trucks equipped with sleeping quarters for the crew, designed to haul giant containers. Container-carrying freight planes the size of a football field. A space-saving airport that is nearly all underground. Ultralight, one-passenger planes. A one-person recreational submarine propelled by an electric-powered tail section that is jointed so it can wriggle like a fish's tail. A multistory hovercraft hotel that cruises over land and water on a cushion of air, settling on either as directed by its captain-manager and a computer. One idea leads to another—to floating cities, to passenger spaceships, to islands in the sky . . . .

There will always be those who say it can't be done. Dreamers Workshop is like many such workshops that exist throughout the world, in major corporations, laboratories, think tanks, backyard barns, basements, and garages. In these places, "dreamers" are dealing with the art of making possibilities come true. They are using imagination and brains and technology to turn what seem to be wild-eyed schemes into reality. For every person who declares a thing to be impossible, there is another who does it.

CHAPTER 3

From Wheels to Wings

For thousands upon thousands of years the speed of travel did not change. Whatever the foot-power used—man, woman, child, ox, donkey, or any other cooperative animal—getting there was slow and tiring work. The fastest means of long-distance land travel was the camel caravan. On a good day a convoy of the "ships of the desert" might average about two and a half miles an hour.

Even the dazzling discovery of the wheel by that unknown Sumerian didn't speed things up very much. The first crude carts and wagons, running on solid round discs, made traveling much more convenient, but they could barely go as fast as a caravan. Then, in about 2000 B.C., the Babylonians designed a new spoked wheel to replace the solid disc. It made for a lighter cart more suitable to the speed of the horse than the lumbering strength of the ox. Along the way, the maneuverable wagon was put to use as a war chariot, and in this form managed a top speed of about twenty miles an hour.

Improvements in both the wheel and the chariot followed down through the centuries, and some very elegant and beautiful carriages came into use. The pace of travel, however, remained much the same. No horse or team of horses could be made to move any faster. Fifteen to twenty miles per hour was, for thousands of years, the ultimate rate of movement for the average traveler.

The coming of steam was actually a step backward. In 1825, the world's first steam-powered freight and passenger service began on the Stockton and Darlington Railway in England. To the accompaniment of loud applause from about forty thousand onlookers, several brass bands, the clanging of church bells, and the salutes of seven

For those who think traffic jams are a recent development, here is a view of Forest Park in St. Louis, Missouri, on a Sunday afternoon in 1920.

eighteen-pound cannons, the engine and its wagonloads of intrepid passengers chugged into Stockton after a razzle-dazzle run of . . . four miles per hour.

"What can be more palpably absurd and ridiculous," sneered the *Quarterly Review* of March 1825, "than the prospect held out of locomotives travelling twice as fast as stage coaches!"

It is only fair to add that, four and a half years later, a competition between several locomotives produced a winner—the Stephenson Rocket—that, in a series of increasingly thrilling laps, produced a top speed of twenty-nine miles per hour.

Only in the last half of the nineteenth century did railroaders develop vastly improved steam locomotives capable of reaching a hundred miles per hour.

Consider the millions of years it had taken to reach that point.

A camel caravan passes near the Red Sea on its slow journey between Egypt and Mesopotamia, below. A Mesopotamian spoke-wheeled chariot, such as the one at right, moved ten times as fast as the caravan.

Yet, less than forty years after the turn of the century, the speed of the fastest train was more than quadrupled by a craft that traveled through the air. Within the next two decades the record was easily doubled. Starting in the late '1950s and throughout the 1960s, supersonic aircraft reached speeds of forty-five hundred miles per hour—and climbing. And by the 1960s, spacecraft were looping around the earth at eighteen thousand miles per hour.

Millions of years to reach a hundred miles per hour . . . less than a century to achieve eighteen thousand.

It seems unlikely that mankind will be able to keep up the momentum of the middle years of the twentieth century. But this has been a period marked by many technological breakthroughs, and the trend cannot help but continue to sweep us along. After so many small steps and giant leaps, mankind will not stand still for thousands of years, waiting for a wheel or a faster horse or a better engine to happen along. Looking at future progress in the light of what the human race has already achieved, we can hardly conceive of anything that we may not do one day.

Rolling on Roads

Roads began, as most things have begun, when mankind found a need for them. Hunters tracking game, traders tracking trade, warriors tracking other warriors, migrants fleeing famine or seeking freedom—all traveled paths that became our first roads.

It was probably the Chinese of the Chou dynasty who, beginning before 1000 B.C., developed the first planned, permanent road system in history. But it was definitely the Romans who constructed the world's first great, durable network of highways. Parts of the Appian Way, built by a Roman official, Appius Claudius Caecus (the Blind), in 312 B.C., are still usable today. At the end of some six hundred years of road construction, which included the building of bridges, canals, aqueducts, sidewalks, and drainage gutters, the total mileage produced was equal to a highway that could circle the world ten times. In fact, the Roman road system linked the Roman Empire together from the

Sahara Desert to Scotland, and from Spain to the Euphrates River in the Middle East (as we know the place-names today). By A.D. 200, horse-drawn Roman wheels were rolling over 53,658 miles of main roads, hauling passengers, mail, and freight at a rate of from fifteen to seventy-five miles a day, depending on the load.

But with the decline and fall of the Roman Empire, the great highway system was neglected. Paving stones were hauled away to be used as construction materials, fences, and boundary markers; bridges collapsed and were not rebuilt. Only the two-wheeled cart could travel over the rough ground. Trade shifted to the emerging Arabian empire in the Middle East and Africa. Arab merchants traveled by ship through the Mediterranean and by camel caravan on the roads of North Africa and Asia. The vast transportation system of Europe, and with it the development of advanced wheeled carriages for paved roads, seemed sure to die out.

But, gradually, Europe recovered from the lack of progress in the Middle Ages and entered a period of new growth. New vehicles were seen on the crumbling roads. Various types of four-wheeled carriages began to appear toward the end of the sixteenth century. In their most elegant form, these carriages were covered with gold and decorated with elaborate curlicues and figurines, and they were used only by royalty or the very rich. But beneath the gold and decoration the basic coach was not much more than a box with open sides, set on the springless frame. Passengers, usually two to four of them, sat nose to nose on facing seats, bouncing and swaying in uncomfortable rhythm with the jouncing of the coach. Springs, brakes, and rubber tires were added to provide some small measure of comfort.

In towns and cities, these four-wheelers continued to transport only the privileged few. But by the eighteenth century the roads in both England and the new world of America had improved enough to encourage popular travel between cities some distance apart. In 1640, the first regular stagecoach service was inaugurated. A century later, a trip on a "flying coach" between London and Manchester, a distance of about four hundred miles, took four and a half days. In 1756, the first stagecoach line in the United States began service between New York and Philadelphia. Typically, a coach carried six to fourteen passengers, their baggage, the mail, and a driver, and was drawn by four to six horses, which were changed at relay stations along the way. At the end of a twelve-hour day, the weary passengers would stagger off for refreshment and rest, having traveled, in good weather, perhaps one hundred miles. The fare: about a nickel a mile.

From about 1725, the farmers of the Conestoga region of Pennsylvania had used heavy covered wagons, drawn by teams of horses, to carry their loads of produce to distant markets. Soon after the westward movement began in the early nineteenth century, Conestoga wagons were carrying goods across the Alleghenies to western frontier settlements and stores. In 1841, when the great westbound migration to Missouri and points beyond got under way, the pioneers rode across the mountains and the Great Plains in "prairie schooners," which were versions of the Pennsylvania farmers' wagons. Neither royalty nor the very rich were among the passengers.

Meanwhile, in 1827, the poorer people of Paris had begun riding through their city's streets in licensed, horse-drawn omnibuses, which soon became known simply as buses. They next appeared in London in 1829 and in New York City in 1830, usually in the double-decker form, with passengers riding both inside and on the roof.

By that time, in what was thought of as the civilized world, a lot of people thought that we had gone about as far as we could go.

The "Iron Horse" Is Born

But there were those who wanted the horses to go faster. The horses couldn't. Even in 1857, the stagecoach run from St. Louis to San Francisco took twenty-five days of round-the-clock travel. There had to be another way.

And there was.

Some fifty years earlier, shortly after the birth of the nineteenth century, an American inventor and steam-engine builder named Oliver Evans had looked into the future and declared: "The time will come when people will travel by steam engines, from one city to another, almost as fast as birds fly. A carriage will set out from Washington in the morning, the passenger will breakfast at Baltimore, dine in Philadelphia, and sup in New York the same day."

Not everyone found the prospect totally appealing, but the forecast was well-founded. The Scottish inventor James Watt had already, in 1769, patented a practical steam engine for industry and given thought to "the application of the steam engine . . . to driving wheel carriages." (He had also coined the term *horsepower;* and the *watt,* a unit of electrical power, was named for him.)

Watt's own steam engines, though they powered machines in factories and mills, were too big and clumsy and did not build up enough pressure to be used in wheeled vehicles. A more likely device appeared on the scene at about that same time, when a French army engineer named Nicolas Joseph Cugnot designed and built a steam-powered wheeled vehicle that puffed along at slightly better than two miles per hour. Its leisurely pace blinded many to its great promise, and Cugnot's achievement went nowhere.

Yet the steam revolution had begun. Oliver Evans, one of its earliest pioneers, built several high-pressure engines that improved on the inventions of Watt and Cugnot and could propel land vehicles on turnpike roads and city streets. But when he tried selling them to coachmakers and others who might be interested, he was unsuccessful. Never, he complained, did he find "a person willing to contribute to the expense or even encourage me." Evans gave up on road machines and concentrated his talents on designing stationary, high-pressure steam engines for industry.

Other inventors carried on. In 1801, a boisterous Cornishman named Richard Trevithick built a high-pressure steam carriage, which he chose to test during Christmas week. He and a group of

John Gast's allegorical *Spirit of the Frontier, 1872,* portrays not only the pioneering spirit of America but the various means of travel to the West, including covered wagon, stagecoach, and train.

London, 1860s: Standing room only on a "Knifeboard" omnibus, named for the narrow bench on the roof.

friends boarded the carriage and took off up a hill, achieving in that moment the distinction of being the first passengers to be transported by steam power. The experience was short-lived. Trevithick's machine broke down somewhere on the hill.

Trevithick then set out to build a new and vastly improved machine. On test runs in London, the vehicle reached a speed of eight miles per hour on the city streets. Off he went to Wales, to try it on tracks. In February 1804, his steam locomotive, pulling a train of five wagons carrying seventy passengers and ten tons of iron, made its first run on tracks. It puffed over a cast-iron tramway connecting an iron foundry to the Glamorganshire Canal, becoming the world's first freight and passenger train.

Finally, Trevithick, like Evans, became discouraged. Neither industry nor the general public realized the possibilities of his creation. Ironically, the

Cugnot's two-mile-per-hour road engine, 1769

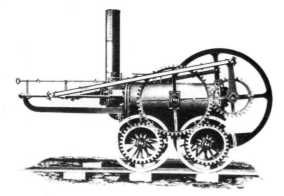

The Trevithick railway locomotive, 1804

Locomotion No. 1, Stockton and Darlington, 1825

The Stephenson Rocket, 1829

main drawback to its practical use was the nature of existing tracks. They were all of cast iron, which is brittle. The weight of the early locomotives caused so many breakages and breakdowns that the mine owners, who also owned the tracks and were the only possible customers for a railroad engine, rejected the "iron horse" as impractical.

But another Englishman, George Stephenson of Northumberland, had firm faith in the future of the railway steam locomotive. Born in a mining district, employed on mines throughout his boyhood, he used his talent for tinkering with machines to such good purpose that he was made the engineer at the Killingworth Colliery in 1812. In July 1814, his five-ton steam locomotive Blucher, hauling a thirty-ton load of eight wagons, rolled without mishap over the coal mine's tramway.

For the next several years Stephenson continued to improve his engines, confident that a public display would prove their worth. His chance came in the 1820s, when he was appointed engineer of the new Stockton and Darlington Railway and was free to do much as he pleased.

Initially, he planned to run his latest-model locomotive on three-foot cast-iron rails of his own design. But it came to his attention that one John Bitkinshaw, of the Bedlington Ironworks at Morpeth, had developed wrought-iron rails in fifteen-foot lengths, which would permit a far superior track.

Stephenson laid a twelve-mile wrought-iron track for the Stockton and Darlington Railway and inaugurated it on September 27, 1825, with a three-hour run of his pioneer Locomotion. There were some cheers, but not many. The locomotive's boilers could not produce a large enough head of steam for continuous high-speed work and proved suitable for only very slow-speed hauling.

The engine's performance was so unimpressive that the Stockton and Darlington line continued to use horses to draw their passenger coaches. George Stephenson's next clients, the owners of the Liverpool and Manchester line, wanted to haul trains along by ropes, pulled by stationary engines working in relays along the sides of the track.

New York Central's Twentieth Century Limited about to depart Grand Central Station for Chicago in 1925. Below right: The train passes Lake Erie.

Stephenson would have none of this, nor would his son Robert. "Rely upon it," wrote Robert to his father, "locomotives should not be cowardly given up. I will fight for them until the last. They are worthy of a conflict." It was he who designed the Rocket, which achieved the triumphant speed of twenty-nine miles per hour in October 1829.

Thus, when the Liverpool and Manchester line opened for business in 1830 with its all-new wrought-iron tracks and its Stephenson locomotives, it became the first railway in the world to rely exclusively on steam engines. Overland transport would no longer be limited to the speed of a horse or a team of animals. Bad weather and poor roads were no longer great obstacles. Coal-hauling charges dropped dramatically. Passenger travel turned from the roads to the rails.

The "iron horse" was on its way.

Across the Atlantic, the British-made Stourbridge Lion made a trial run at ten miles per hour on a track in Pennsylvania in August 1829. American engineers went into high gear and produced a dozen new locomotives in the space of a year.

Speed and efficiency increased. Short-run railroads began to appear throughout the United States. By 1836, more than 1,200 miles of track had been completed; by 1850, 9,021 miles; by 1860, 30,626 miles. The first transcontinental line was begun in 1863, with the Union Pacific building westward from Omaha and the Central Pacific reaching eastward from Sacramento. The two roads were joined at Promontory, Utah, on May 10, 1869, and a telegraph flashed the message: "The last rail is laid. The last spike is driven. The Pacific Railroad is completed."

Time and the talents of many men had transformed the tiny rattletrap locomotives of the early nineteenth century into the 700,000-pound giants able to haul hundred-car freight trains over the Rockies. From country to country, the great trains appeared and revolutionized the transportation

The General, a wood-burning locomotive, was used in the Civil War. It was restored in the 1960s (left).

33

Three famous early automobiles, from left: the 1887 Benz three-wheeler, world's first automobile; the first Stanley Steamer, 1897; the first Ford Model-T of 1908—the no-frills car for the masses.

systems of the world. As speeds reached eighty, ninety, a hundred miles per hour, steel roads replaced iron ones and diesel-electric power replaced steam. The magnificent railroad train became even more magnificent—until a different kind of vehicle came along.

The Automobile Takes Over

When Nicolas Cugnot, Oliver Evans, and Richard Trevithick developed their first steam-driven carriages, they ran them not on tracks but on cobbled city streets and unpaved country roads. No one thought of the devices as horseless carriages, much less automobiles. But that is what they were —self-propelled vehicles capable of carrying passengers.

Many other vehicles like these were developed in England during the next hundred years. But the road coaches were never fully accepted by the authorities, who did not think they were safe.

Yet steam was on the roads. It might well have become the power source for individual motorized transport if Nikolaus Otto of Germany had not developed a four-cycle internal combustion engine *(see Glossary)*. Otto put his engine, fueled by gasoline, on the market in 1876. A decade later, Gottfried Daimler and Karl Benz used engines of the Otto type in, respectively, a four-wheeled vehicle and a three-wheeler. The Daimler and Benz machines were the first horseless carriages designed for personal use. They were simple and fragile. In 1894, the Daimler company introduced to the world the larger, more substantial Panhard car— which even then had many characteristics of the modern automobile.

A new age in transport was on the horizon.

In the United States, the first internal combustion automobiles of the horseless carriage type were built in the 1890s by the Duryea twins, Charles and Frank, of Chicopee, Massachusetts. The brothers never achieved more than modest fame for their pioneering efforts. But their cars

A steam-driven autobus, used in France in the 1890s, about to be passed by a man on a tricycle.

were almost the equal of the European imports and set an American standard for such men as Ransom E. Olds and Henry Ford.

Foreign cars such as the then-roomy Italian Fiat, Germany's fast Mercedes (named after a girl called Mercedes Jellinek), and England's luxurious Rolls-Royce Silver Ghost were virtually custom-built . . . and costly. American automobile manufacturers wanted a wider market. In 1906, Ransom Olds began mass-producing America's first low-priced car, which would soon be immortalized in song as "My Merry Oldsmobile." The crop of new vehicles prompted a somewhat unfair comment from Woodrow Wilson, then president of Princeton University and later president of the United States. Wilson complained that the car was "a picture of the arrogance of wealth." The merry Olds arrogant?

Perhaps it was not quite yet the people's car, but the American automobile very soon became the vehicle of choice for the average person. This happened when an even more affordable car than the Olds began to emerge by the thousands from a factory in Detroit. It was the 20-h.p. Model-T Ford, or "Tin Lizzie" as some called it, designed and mass-produced by Henry Ford. His approach was to keep manufacturing costs low by using the conveyor belt and assembly line for automobile production. He concentrated on a standardized, open-doored, no-frills car—"Any customer can have a car painted any color he wants, so long as it is black"—and outbuilt, outpriced, and outsold all his competitors. More than fifteen million Model-Ts had been sold, some for under three hundred dollars, by the time the model was discontinued and a new Model-A went into production in 1928.

Meanwhile, there had been other interesting developments in the automotive field. Back in 1839, a Scotsman, Robert Anderson, had built the first of a series of cars that ran on stored electricity. Many thousands more were built through the late nineteenth and early twentieth centuries. During this time the electric car became the first vehicle to achieve a speed of sixty miles an hour. Its major drawback was that it could only travel a short distance before it had to stop for recharging.

A Kansas family pauses proudly for a photograph before taking a ride in an elegant 1903 Cadillac.

This major electrical problem might have been solved in time had it not been for another invention that made a battery-powered car a thing of the past. This was an electric self-starter for gasoline engines, devised by Charles F. Kettering some years before he went to work for General Motors. The awkward, often dangerous hand crank was no longer necessary. It was replaced by a device that enabled a person to step into a car and start it by turning a switch and pressing a button.

The short-range electric vehicle lost ground to the more convenient and practical gasoline-powered car, and fell by the wayside in the late 1920s.

A steam-powered car, on the other hand, almost made it.

The Stanley brothers, Francis and Freelan, of Massachusetts began producing their Stanley Steamers in 1897 and continued production through World War I. At one time—1906—the Stanley steam car was the fastest in the world, having broken all existing records with a speed of 127.66 miles per hour. But ultimately the electrically started internal combustion machine outdid the Steamer in low cost, high reliability, and popular appeal.

"Four Letters: A-U-T-O"

"Why on earth do you need to study what's changing the country?" a sociologist was asked in Indiana in the 1920s. "I can tell you what's happening in just four letters: A-U-T-O."

From the start, automobiles were far more than just a means of transportation. They brought to even the most humdrum of lives a real sense of freedom and mobility. ("The car is the only pleasure we have," one working woman said.) Cars were also status symbols, to be prized, polished and pampered. A young man might not be able to afford a luxurious Cadillac, Pierce-Arrow, or Packard, but there were plenty of less expensive models. And when he took his girl for a ride in his Chevrolet, he felt every bit as dashing as a movie star in a Duesenberg.

Cars changed almost everything—dating habits, vacations, where we worked and lived. Will Rogers, the humorist, had a suggestion for churches suffering declining attendance: hold services on "days when they are fixing the roads, and they will pack 'em in."

In the 1930s, Cadillac offered thirty variations of its luxurious V-16, above, with many custom features, all for prices ranging from $5,350 to $15,000. Clark Gable chose a Packard Twin Six roadster, below.

Ransom Olds, with an eye on the mass market, built a light but sturdy car and proclaimed its virtues and safety compared to "the danger of the horse's uncertain temper, sudden fright, and unruly disposition." The free advertising provided by a hit song, "In My Merry Oldsmobile" (left), helped boost sales. The Chevrolet, or "Chevy" as it is known to Americans, also became and remained an affordable favorite. Below, a couple proudly pose with their Chevrolet sedan, vintage 1940. Above is a drawing of a jaunty 1953 Chevrolet Corvette, America's first production sports car, which had a six-cylinder engine and an automatic transmission.

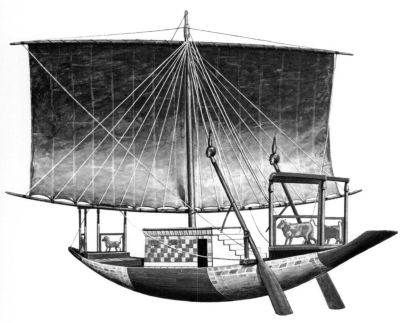

While the Ford factories retooled for the Model-A, which would remain the Ford model for several years, General Motors initiated a new concept in automobile production: the annual model change.

Americans loved the idea. Many of them bought a new car every year. Automobile manufacturing and merchandising were revolutionized. Roads, cities, and rural areas experienced startling changes as more and more people bought cars. The American passion for the railroad train was put aside in favor of a new love object: the gasoline-engine automobile.

Exploring the World's Waterways

The wheel and steam also came to have their uses on the waterways of the world. But this happened only many thousands of years after transportation by sea had become both a practical science and an art . . . as well as an easy way to use nature as a source of power.

Waterborne travelers had much less need of invention than those traveling on land. Road building was not required because the water itself was the road. A ready source of energy existed in the currents, in human arms, and in the wind. The boat was supported by the water and floated on the surface no matter what its size, so that bigger and better boats could be built without the problems of support and friction that concerned the builders of land vehicles. Logs, reeds, hides, and

Huge oars at the stern were used to steer the Egyptian sailboat above, which sailed on the Nile around 2000 B.C. The galley at right was used by the Roman navy to dominate the Mediterranean Sea. Propelled primarily by rows of oars, it also had a large sail that was used when the winds were favorable. Among the features used in battle were the bronze-covered ram at the bow, catapults, turrets for archers, and a corvus, or hooked drawbridge, used to board enemy ships. Light and fast, the galley had a continuous keel. Its ribbed frame was covered with tar-coated wood planking.

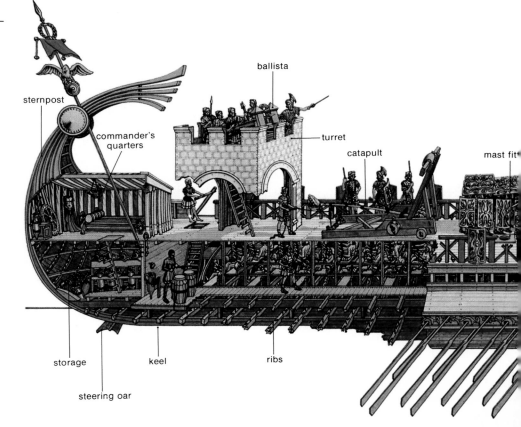

sternpost
commander's quarters
ballista
turret
catapult
mast fit
storage
keel
ribs
steering oar

other raw materials were readily available and easily carved or molded into shape. Wooden rafts, hollowed logs, and skin canoes almost certainly appeared in the waters of the world long before the wheel began to tame the land.

The first civilizations developed near the coasts of warm seas and navigable rivers. By 3000 B.C., the Egyptians flourished in the valley of the Nile, the "long river between the deserts." They used large seagoing cargo boats, based on the craft that traveled the great river, to haul their trade goods to other waters. Over the next two thousand years, their neighbors, the Phoenicians of the Mediterranean, established the first great land-sea system of transportation. They sailed their vessels into seaports connected with caravan routes and thus with inland cities. Phoenician ships were

corvus

ram

outrigger

oars

much like those of the Egyptians, solidly built for strength rather than speed and using oars as well as sails. Their cargoes were luxury goods such as spices, gems, perfumes, and exotic creatures. To King Solomon's great Hebrew kingdom came "ships of Tarshish bringing gold, and silver, ivory, and apes, and peacocks."

Phoenician, Carthaginian, and Greek mariners, looking for new possibilities for trade and expansion, explored the farther reaches of the Mediterranean, the northern coast of Africa, and the Black Sea. At the height of its empire, Rome established sea trade links with India, Ceylon, and China.

Various combinations of oars and sails were attempted throughout the centuries as merchants and adventurers explored the seas, made fortunes, lost lives, and found new worlds. But ship design evolved very slowly. The accepted sources of driving energy were strong rowing arms or a wind in the sails. Shipbuilders and seamen did not search for other, more efficient ways to propel their ships. By the time Portugal and Spain became the leading sea powers in the late Middle Ages, the only changes in ships were improved masts and oars.

Henry the Navigator, prince of Portugal, was no seaman himself. But as a patron of exploration he contributed notably to the art of navigation and the progress of marine transportation. Early in the fifteenth century, he established a school of geography and discovery at Sagres in southwest Portugal—literally, a training center for budding explorers. Under his direction, Henry's captains mapped the west coast of Africa and brought back gold and slaves, which made further African voyages extremely popular. This exploration served to end a great deal of myth and false information about the land and seas of the "dark continent."

Portuguese exploration continued after Henry's death. In 1487, Bartholomeu Dias rounded the southern tip of Africa past the Cape of Good Hope —whose rough weather led him to rename it Cabo Tormentoso, or Cape of Storms. This voyage opened the sea route from Europe to India. A decade later, Vasco da Gama completed the voyage to the Indian coast. The prospects for trade were so promising that the Portuguese sent many more ships to India. Ten years later, Ferdinand

Puffing smoke from its chimneys, the paddle-wheeler *Princess* and another riverboat sail down the Mississippi (above). Fulton's *Clermont,* seen below on its maiden voyage of 1807, was the first steamboat to be commercially successful in America.

Magellan found a short cut from the Atlantic to the Pacific and a sea route around the world.

Meanwhile, a Genoese mariner in the Portuguese merchant service, Christopher Columbus, had come to believe it was possible to reach what he called the "Indies" by sailing west, a theory that depended on a notion that the world was round. After years of effort, he managed to persuade King Ferdinand and Queen Isabella of Spain to sponsor his enterprise. The result was the voyage in 1492 of the *Nina,* the *Pinta,* and the *Santa Maria* and the ultimate discovery of a whole new world, which Spain lost no time exploring and conquering.

With the destruction of the Spanish Armada in 1588 by the forces of England's Queen Elizabeth I, Spain lost its position as the leading sea power. By that time, the English seafarer Sir Francis Drake had sailed around the globe and, in 1579, claimed Spanish-occupied California for his queen. In the coming decades, the sea traffic between England and the New World confirmed English dominance of the seas.

Steam Comes to the Seas

Americans would also build ships: frigates, schooners, clipper ships, things of streamlined beauty and graceful sail. The wind was their propelling force. And the wind could drive a clipper to China faster than anything else at sea.

But not more economically. The clipper had yard upon yard of sail, requiring a large crew, and its cargo space was reduced by its narrow, racing lines. Even as it reached its peak it was about to be replaced. The steam engine had arrived in the waters of the New World.

Several steamboats were built and successfully tested on American rivers in the 1780s and 1790s. But it was the *Clermont,* creation of inventor Robert Fulton of Lancaster, Pennsylvania, that first achieved commercial success. Launched in 1807, the *Clermont* was a splendid 150 feet long—almost twice the length of an Egyptian ship of 1300 B.C.—but hardly a speedboat. The 150-mile trip from New York City to Albany took her thirty-two hours; the return trip, thirty. The current and wind being with it, the Egyptian ship might very well have done better.

Yet the steamboat was deemed to be a success, and in 1819 steampower took to the sea in the shape of the American vessel *Savannah*, powered not only by sails but by wheels—side-wheel paddles doing the work of propellers.

In 1845, the *Great Britain*, a huge iron ship that was all steam and no sails, became the first ship to be driven across the Atlantic by a rear-mounted screw propeller, which would soon replace paddle wheels altogether on oceangoing vessels.

But not yet on the steamboats of the great waterways of the American West. Not on the 2,700-mile Missouri River, known as the "Big Muddy" to the rivermen, and not on the Mississippi, nor the Red River, nor the Des Moines.

The steamboat came to the Missouri in 1819 in the form of a side-wheeler designed by Robert Fulton and introduced to the Mississippi eight

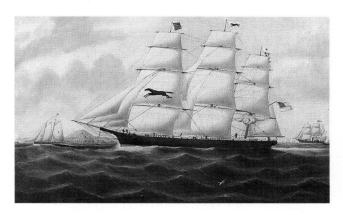

Ship Galatea, a nineteenth-century painting by an unknown artist, depicts a clipper ship under full sail, its sharp bow cleaving the waves (above). The sleek, twenty-knot-per-hour clippers were eventually eclipsed by the ocean liners, such as the elegant *Queen Mary,* below.

The "QUEEN MARY"

THE FIRST CUNARDER "BRITANNIA" TOGETHER WITH THE THREE SHIPS WITH WHICH COLUMBUS FIRST CROSSED THE ATLANTIC COULD BE PLACED IN THE MAIN FOYER *and* RESTAURANT *of* The "QUEEN MARY"

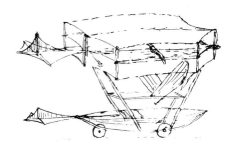

years before. According to one river skipper, it was "the most beautiful creation of man." Beautiful it was, but underpowered and needing six feet of water to proceed.

This was much too deep for the shallower areas of the Big Muddy. Changes were made to increase the vessel's range, and the true Missouri riverboat eventually emerged in 1859: a rugged stern-wheeler with a powerful engine and a load capacity of 350 tons. It needed only two and a half feet to ease it over the shifting sandbars and hidden obstacles of the Missouri.

But then the railroads began to take over the work of the Big Muddy and its boats and rivermen, and within thirty years the glory days of the paddle-wheel steamboat were over.

Fashionable Spanish ladies and gentlemen gather to watch the ascent of a Montgolfier hot-air balloon over Madrid in the mid-1780s.

At sea, the great days of the ocean liners were about to begin. By the 1880s, regular Atlantic crossings were being made by passenger ships. Their engines, with twenty-eight thousand horsepower and more, would soon be overtaken by a new development—turbine steampower. This advance provided even more efficient engines for the great liners of the 1930s, 1940s, and 1950s: the *Queen Mary,* the *Queen Elizabeth,* and the *United States.* The last, the most ambitious ship in American history, generated 240,000 horsepower and was capable of a speed of up to forty knots. In 1952, it made a 2,949-mile crossing of the Atlantic in the record time of three days, ten hours, and forty minutes, beating the previous record by ten hours and two minutes.

But that speed across the Atlantic had already been beaten by an altogether different type of passenger craft.

The First Attempts to Fly

Leonardo da Vinci, great Italian genius of the Renaissance, was convinced that man had the ability "to sustain himself in the air by the flapping of wings." From the 1480s until his death in 1519, Leonardo tried to design a flyable craft.

Man had shared da Vinci's belief for hundreds of years, and had gone so far as to test it by leaping off towers in a great variety of feathered cloaks and strapped-on wings. Many casualties had resulted. All the birdmen and tower jumpers failed to understand the nature of bird flight, which does not depend on wing flapping alone. As later bird watchers realized, it depended on the lifting action of the air as it rushed over cambered, or arched, wings and on the way wingtip feathers were used to provide forward motion. In addition, after many painful failures, it became clear that man's weight and body strength are not designed for lifting and propelling him like a bird.

Leonardo made hundreds of designs for muscle-powered "ornithopters," or wing-flapping craft. But these must rank among the least practi-

Germany's Otto Lilienthal soars over the heads of spectators on a flight in 1894. With his heavier than-air devices, he achieved glides of a thousand feet.

cal of his works. And yet he foresaw a helicopter-like machine with a screw-type propeller that would make it "spiral in the air and . . . rise high." He also sketched a parachute and a number of unflyable winged craft that came very close to suggesting solutions to some of the problems of flight.

But Leonardo's work remained unpublished and had no influence on other thinkers. Would-be fliers continued to try out unworkable contraptions and new schemes.

And then, in 1783, the brothers Joseph and Etienne Montgolfier, papermakers of the French town of Antonnay, discovered that a paper bag filled with heated air will rise from the ground. In June of that year they staged a public demonstration of their first unmanned lighter-than-air craft. It was a huge paper-lined linen balloon that rose to a height of six thousand feet and drifted on the wind for ten minutes before alighting a mile from its takeoff point. A few months later they staged another launching, this time before the court of Louis XVI at Versailles, sending aloft a duck, a cock, and a sheep in a basket attached to the balloon. Then, in November, two passengers—not the brothers—climbed into a larger basket, or gondola, and were carried five miles across the city of Paris by the marvelous balloon of the Montgolfiers.

It seemed as if the age of flight had at last arrived, especially when other inventors began using hydrogen as a lifting gas instead of hot air. Ballooning then developed into a craze that would culminate in the airships of the 1920s and 1930s. But the lighter-than-air enthusiasts had not discovered the secret of true, birdlike powered flight.

A clue to that secret already existed in the kite, known in the Orient for thousands of years and frequently used for aerial observation and as a signaling device. Occasionally, a kite even carried a man aloft to test the weather. But it was not until the early years of the nineteenth century that someone with a questioning mind understood the true significance of the windborne kite. It was a heavier-than-air device capable of lifting more than its own weight, and it could be controlled in

Orville and Wilbur Wright, above, made their dream of flight come true on December 17, 1903. Below, Wilbur watches as Orville takes the *Flyer* aloft.

various ways. The kite was, in fact, man's best version of a bird, and in its simple form demonstrated the basic principles of flight.

Sir George Cayley, a Yorkshire baronet, spent most of his life attempting to develop a heavier-than-air flying machine modeled on the kite form and propelled by a mechanical power system. In 1804, he built his first aircraft, a model glider with fixed wings and a tail unit that provided control and stability. It sailed so well that he used its basic form in a number of full-size gliders. Occasionally, these left the ground for several yards at a time.

Alternately studying soaring birds and experimenting with model wing shapes in his workshed, Sir George learned the importance of streamlined forms and arched wings. He also discovered the propellerlike function of the bird's wingtips. He was sure that he was on the right track toward launching a powered aircraft. "The whole problem is confined within these limits," he wrote, "to make a surface support a given weight by the application of power to the resistance of the air."

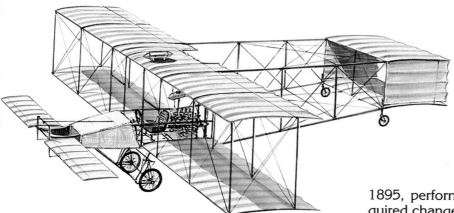

Henri Farman, an Englishman living in France, began producing biplanes such as this one in 1909.

Cayley came close to solving that problem, yet finally failed. He was the first researcher to spell out the principles and practical use of aerodynamics *(see Glossary)*. And he was the first to succeed in lifting a flying machine into the air. But he could not find a source of power for forward motion. The only power system available in his time was the steam engine, and that was too clumsy and heavy for use in an aircraft.

Yet the English baronet's work inspired not only other Englishmen but European and American inventors as well. Several of these inventors developed promising machines that glided for short distances or made steampowered hops that could not be repeated. Lightweight power was simply not there. To Germany's Otto Lilienthal, the answer was to continue studying bird flight and to perfect his gliding technique in a series of increasingly advanced machines, while experimenting with power sources on the side.

During the 1890s, Lilienthal made more than two thousand flights on a type of hang-glider. He controlled the glider by shifting his body weight, and some of his flights were well over a thousand feet long, a spectacular achievement at a time when men who tried to fly were thought to be fools. "One can get a proper insight into the practice of flying only by actual experiments," Lilienthal wrote in 1896. "The manner in which we have to meet the irregularities of the wind, when soaring in the air, can only be learned by being in the air itself."

Yet in spite of his extensive study of birds and his own experience in the air, he still did not fully understand powered flight. In 1893, he started work on a powered glider with a carbonic-acid gas motor that was supposed to make the wingtips flap and drive the aircraft forward. His first model failed to leave the ground, and the second, built in

1895, performed poorly in its first trials and required changes before being retested.

Had he been able to test his new machines thoroughly, Lilienthal would have realized that they could not work. But on August 9, 1896, he ran into a sudden gust of wind while making a routine flight in one of his unpowered gliders and went into a stall that he was unable to correct. He died the next day of a broken spine.

Later experimenters would realize, as had Cayley, that flapping wings were not the answer to the question of propulsion, or forward power.

Nonetheless, Lilienthal left two major gifts to his fellow aeronauts: a solid body of evidence that it was possible to glide through the air in a heavier-than-air machine and a number of written works, including a book called *Birdflight as the Basis of Aviation,* which became the bible of aeronautical literature.

The Invention of Powered Flight

Among those who were influenced by Lilienthal's work were two inspired mechanics and aviation enthusiasts, Wilbur and Orville Wright of Dayton, Ohio.

When Lilienthal made his last glider flight in 1896, the Wright Cycle Company was doing a booming business in the manufacture, repair, and sale of the Wright brothers' bicycles. Always interested in gadgets and machines, Wilbur and Orville were fascinated with Lilienthal's research. They responded to the challenge of flight by researching everything ever written on the subject. Like those who came before them, they studied the wing movements of the bird. The soaring birds, they observed, did not flap their wings but glided until a wind gust flipped them out of balance. At that point, they would right themselves with a slight twisting of the wingtips.

In 1899, they began experimenting with kites, concentrating on the development of a system to control the kites' movement. Then came a series of experiments with kitelike gliders, which they test-flew—when their business was slow—over the sand dunes of Kill Devil Hills on North Carolina's Outer Banks. Back in Dayton, they tackled the problems of flight, one after another. They conducted wind tunnel tests in their workshop to determine the aerodynamic shape for their glider's wings. They devised a system of twisting the wings to maintain the balance of their machine and bank it into turns. They provided a horizontal front-end rudder, or elevator, to control its climb and descent. And they designed subtly arched wings to improve its lifting capacity.

Finally, with the gasoline engines of Daimler and Benz to guide them, they built their own 12-h.p. aircraft engine. Then, inspired by the screw propellers used on ships, they fashioned their own pusher-type propellers. For the first time in man's long dream of flight, all the elements had been brought together.

On December 17, 1903, watched by a little band of spectators from a nearby lifesaving station, Wilbur and Orville set their powered glider upon its track and took turns at its controls.

Many times before, depending on the air currents, they had glided farther than their longest engine-propelled flight of that day—a distance of 852 feet, in the time aloft of fifty-nine seconds. But what they did that day was historic. Never before in the history of the world had a controllable, man-carrying machine raised itself into the air by its own power, sailed forward well above the ground without losing speed, and landed at a point as high as that from which it had started.

It was some time before the world outside realized that the Wright brothers' first few flights marked the beginning of a new era in the history of the world. But the observers at Kill Devil Hills knew what they had seen. "They have done it! They have done it!" yelled one witness, racing to the nearby Kitty Hawk post office with the incredible news. "They have done it! Damned if they ain't flew!"

It was a simple beginning, but a great one. There was much more to come—bigger, better, faster, higher, hotter, bolder: sailless craft seeking out the new worlds of the universe.

Yet it all began with the wing of the bird, and the men who understood it. The Wrights' first flights of December 1903 were not only man's first hesitant steps into the air. They were man's first ventures into space.

Louis Blériot practices for a 1901 Channel crossing.

The U.S. Army's *Chicago* after a 1924 world flight.

A Douglas DC-3, the leading airliner for 20 years.

America's World War I ace, Eddie Rickenbacker.

A tennis match on the wings of a plane, 1925.

Lindbergh prepares for his 1927 transatlantic solo.

Igor Sikorsky at the controls of a 1940s helicopter.

A World War II Vickers *Supermarine Spitfire.*

X-1 test pilots Chuck Yeager and Arthur Murray.

CHAPTER 4

Moving Ahead on Land

Ransom Olds and Henry Ford had been right. Americans wanted personal transportation. By the hundreds of thousands, and then by the millions, they bought their cars, drove them, and loved them. Their wives and sons and daughters loved them too. They borrowed them, then bought their own.

In 1900, there were about eight thousand automobiles and a few trucks bouncing over American roads, and about ten thousand motor vehicles on the roads worldwide. By 1929, there were twenty-three million cars on American roads, one for every five people.

Almost from the beginning, as historian James Flink says, "automobility quickly became a mass movement in the United States." No other development in the life of a nation has so strongly influenced our national culture and living habits.

The first and most obvious example of the automobile's impact on American society was an increase in travel. In 1914, for example, the average American traveled about 340 miles a year by automobile, horse, buggy, or cycle. By the end of the 1960s, the typical American car owner was logging ten thousand miles a year. Often trips required overnight stays at one's destination or at rest stops along the way.

Hotel business picked up in towns and cities. A new institution swept across the land. It was the motel, from whose humble beginnings would spring a giant new industry. Other enterprises mushroomed nearby: gas stations, fast food stands, small stores selling whatever they thought motorists might buy. Then came full-service gas stations, sit-down restaurants, and various forms of entertainment, from miniature golf ranges to amusement parks.

The Planetran, a sleek magnetic levitation train (Maglev) propelled by electromagnets, could whisk passengers from New York to Los Angeles through underground tunnels in less than an hour.

The long-distance rigs above are parked outside a truck stop. In the future, drivers will sleep and eat in their trucks while computers do the driving.

Inevitably, retailers of all sorts set up shop where people came to play. Groups of stores sprang up along major highways and developers noted their success. They created shopping and service malls that catered to almost every possible consumer desire. The nation's economy changed radically. The nation's life-style was altered forever.

The cause of this upheaval, the automobile industry, became the world's largest manufacturing concern and generated many jobs and much income. Related industries such as tire manufacturing also flourished. Meanwhile, the nation's way of life continued to change. Workers no longer had to live close to factories and other places of business. They could use their cars to drive to work. The outer limits of towns erupted into towering apartment buildings. Beyond the city limits, suburban communities were built. The low-priced car became a family necessity and a family habit. It was the all-purpose, versatile vehicle for getting to the factory or office, running to the supermarket, picking up a date, taking the kids to school, visiting grandma, or going on a vacation.

But, versatile as it was, the standard family car was not suited for every need. The basic form was transformed and refined into sports cars and sta-

tion wagons, pickups and recreation vehicles. Complete homes on wheels rumbled down the highways and parked in trailer camps.

In the area of public transportation, taxicabs and limousines competed with private cars on crowded city streets. The number of urban, suburban, and long-distance buses multiplied, offering inexpensive travel to people without wheels of their own. And the people flowed back and forth across the land.

The movement of goods as well as people was transformed by the development of motorized highway transportation. In the United States today, more freight is carried by motor truck than any other way. Railroads carry goods for longer distances. But trucks haul far greater tonnages over short- and medium-distance routes. And trucks can serve rural routes with great flexibility, carrying goods between locations not served by any other type of freight carrier.

Although very much an American development, "automobility" has proved to be not solely American. By 1981, the world automobile fleet was 331 million, plus 61 million buses and trucks. Of the current worldwide total, about 160 million passenger cars, trucks, and buses are registered in the United States: one vehicle per every 1.4 people—millions and millions of wheels, all needing something to drive on.

Every year, about $30 billion is spent on rebuilding and resurfacing tens of thousands of miles of American roads. Every year, about seventy-five thousand miles of new streets, roads, and highways are added. By the early 1980s, there were 3.9 million miles of roadways, 3.4 million of which were surfaced. The federal highway program begun in the mid-1950s provided many thousands of miles of these roads. Under this program there came into being a network of high-speed highways that contributed greatly to the postwar explosion in auto travel.

The Changing Transportation Scene
Yet all of our millions of wheels and miles of highways are not enough to fill our present and future land transportation needs. Both automobiles and the roads they travel are likely to be

greatly changed within the next two or three decades. Cars will be safer, and save fuel. Pollution will be reduced. Highways will speed traffic through the use of advanced computer controls.

Railroad transportation will also change greatly. Underused or neglected railroad tracks may come into use again. Or they may be replaced by new tracks that can accommodate high-speed trains capable of competing with airline service. Innovations also will occur in urban and suburban transportation systems. For example, short-distance rapid transit services will be developed that will be able to move people far more quickly than automobiles and buses can. These systems will do much to free downtown areas from their present traffic jams.

The potential now exists for the development of advanced types of land transportation in many forms, from better and faster walkways to computer-controlled cars and highways to subterranean cross-country rocket trains.

The changes will not come overnight. For the next twenty to fifty years, the auto will remain the primary form of land transportation. The great challenge of the 1980s and 1990s is to increase the efficiency of our existing highway system and the vehicles that use it. There is another side to this challenge. At the same time that we work on increasing efficiency and capacity, we must focus on three other goals: to conserve our limited supplies of energy, to make auto and truck transportation safer, and to reduce pollution.

To begin with, the challenge is shaped by our astoundingly high level of highway use. The Hollywood Freeway, for example, was supposed to carry traffic totaling 120,000 cars a day by 1970. Yet it was handling twice that much traffic by 1965. Almost always, the roads and highways con-

Houston, Texas, 1983 (below): A swirl of ramps, overpasses and cloverleafs confronts urban drivers.

structed to meet present traffic demands have produced more roadways in both town and country—bigger, better, wider, but mainly *more.*

Yet there is a limit to *more.* Much of the developed world already has a superabundance of highways and turnpikes. There is a growing reluctance to increase road mileage at the expense of rural areas and living space.

The solution is to improve and change existing roads rather than to add new ones. Highways are now being enlarged by what one transportation expert at the Massachusetts Institute of Technology (M.I.T.) in Cambridge, Massachusetts, called "bootlegging" space along existing systems—simply stretching them sideways wherever possible. This process will continue.

Another step is to control highway and street traffic more efficiently. One way to do this is to separate vehicles by their type and their purpose, so that delivery vans and passenger cars don't have to compete for the same space on the roads. Sooner, rather than later, there will be separate but adjoining highways for container trucks, long-distance passenger vehicles, short-run commuter cars, downtown delivery vans, and whatever other special kinds of cars and trucks emerge in the future. This will require major changes in the roadbeds of present highways.

To use both new and old roadways more effectively, we will have to make use of both larger and smaller vehicles. One of the larger vehicles will be a superbus with two or three individual but attached units. This "articulated" bus could carry double or triple the number of passengers buses now carry. Another will be supertrucks of awesome size that will haul the containers of the future. Such trucks will make it possible to carry more goods per man-hour, per engine, and per gallon. Still another will be large group-operated and group-occupied commuter cars.

Smaller vehicles, such as one- and two-passenger commuting cars, will play a major role in future highway travel. And in many areas of the world, safe, fast bicycles will be used widely.

Personal automobiles will continue to be the vehicle of choice for many people. Increased use of highways for freight movement and passenger travel will require new and more advanced ways to control traffic. The emphasis will be on safe and efficient traffic flow. Traffic on city streets and expressways will be controlled electronically. Computers will operate traffic signal networks and broadcast instructions to drivers. This will reduce driver independence under certain circumstances while keeping the traffic flowing smoothly.

One model for a control system is called SAFER, or Systematic Aid to Flow on Existing Roads. It uses computers to collect information about traffic as it flows onto the highway from intersections. The computers transmit the data to a central computer. The central computer then sends commands to individual traffic control devices to alter the timing of lights as needed. SAFER adjusts automatically to changing conditions, from a rush-hour jam to a lane blocked by a disabled car. It routes traffic around crowded points and greatly reduces stop-and-go driving. SAFER thus provides a number of benefits. Trips are shorter and more comfortable. Less fuel is consumed because of decreased stop-and-go traffic. Pollution levels are lowered. And there are fewer rear-end collisions and other accidents.

Collisions may be further reduced by the use of either radar or sonar. A radar unit fitted on the front end of a car can track the car ahead. It sets off a warning signal when the distance between the two cars becomes so close it is unsafe. Similarly, sonar auto units are able to sense the speed and distance of the nearest vehicles and display that information on a dashboard panel.

Highway maintenance, repair, and improvement are ongoing and unending. That means systems must be developed to permit road repair without creating traffic slowdowns and stoppages. One such system is the MORV, or Mobile Overpass Roadway Repair Vehicle. It is a movable bridge with inclined ramps for access by cars. Placed over a road repair area, it permits both work and traffic to proceed smoothly.

New Cars, New Fuels

Will the vehicles that travel these new and improved roadways be different from today's cars? The answer is that in the next twenty years, cars will advance in design, performance, and efficiency of operation. But they will not be changed radically from the cars of today. At the same time, however, work will proceed on the development of new kinds of cars, on concepts and models that are quite different from conventional cars. Surveying future possibilities, engineers and futurists make the following predictions:

• Cars will become more and more electronic. Their ignition, radio, cooling and heating, and other systems will all be activated by the driver's voice command.

• A powerful, nonpolluting electric car is a prime target for researchers. The necessary lightweight superbattery is not yet available. But scientists are coming close to perfecting it. The federal government is backing a long-term, multimillion-dollar development program to come up with safe superbatteries that perform efficiently at low cost. The goal is a personal automobile with a top speed of about sixty miles an hour and a range of three hundred miles.

• Various types of fuel cells have already been used in spacecraft *(see Glossary, Fuel Cells).* They show promise of generating hundreds of times

more power than even the superbatteries. Fuel cells are similar in structure to batteries but different in operation. Basically, fuel cells provide electricity by means of a chemical reaction. But a compact, high-energy fuel cell system for automotive use is unlikely to be operative until some years into the twenty-first century.

• Electric cars equipped with a superflywheel, a new kind of energy-storage system, are another possibility. This energy-storage system could make electric vehicles as convenient and efficient as internal combustion automobiles. Superflywheel electric cars could be on the road well before superbatteries or fuel cells are perfected. The superflywheel was developed by an engineer at Johns Hopkins University in Baltimore, Maryland. It is capable of storing and delivering three times the energy of the lead acid batteries now available.

• Steam-powered vehicles may be back. The Stanley Steamer of generations ago was powered by water vapor. Large amounts of that vapor were lost into the atmosphere. This meant the driver had to make frequent stops to refill the water supply. But the modern steam turbine developed by the Lear Motors Corporation does not lose vapor. It has a closed system in which the vapor condenses into a reusable liquid. Still, much more work needs to be done on perfecting the steam turbine for cars before steam-powered vehicles once again roll down the highway.

Streamlined design of trucks and cars of the future (below) will increase fuel efficiency. At the same time, computerized controls will make driving safer.

A trio of dashing Frenchmen pose with their bicycle built for three during the biking craze of the 1890s.

• Another old engine that may return in modern form is the Stirling. It was invented early in the nineteenth century by the Reverend Robert Stirling but has never been used in an automobile. Unlike the internal combustion engine, the low-emission Stirling depends on the combustion of fuel outside the cylinders to heat a gas inside. The gas then expands to move the piston. The Stirling engine would be able to burn almost any kind of fuel both cleanly and economically. After further tests, a Stirling-engine car might be produced before the end of the 1980s.

As far as future fuels are concerned, gasoline will remain the preferred fuel and the one in greatest supply for the balance of the century. At the same time, fuel mileage will improve, approaching one hundred miles per gallon. Among the reasons for this improvement are: (1) smaller and lighter engines, (2) electronic fuel injection, controlled by a computer, that regulates the precise amount of gasoline going to the carburetor, (3) car bodies that are low-slung and streamlined, with no openings or projections, providing greatly reduced wind resistance.

Supplies of gasoline will be extended through the use of several new fuels, including:
• ethanol, which is a kind of alcohol made from a variety of plants, including grains
• "synfuels," which are synthetic crude oils derived from coal and oil shale
• methane gas, which is made from coal and various agricultural wastes
• hydrogen, which could be supplied, for example, in a hydrogen-air mixture or in liquid form.

Liquid hydrogen appears to be the best possibility for the more distant future—the years after 2000.

Future Wonders on the Highway

Looking farther into the future, we encounter another scenario. It features a vehicle that operates automatically on a speedway that has a buried road cable. This is the beginning of the age of the Compucar.

Settling into her semicomputerized car on a weekday morning, the commuter drives to her office through local suburban streets with her auto set on manual control. Several miles from her home, she leaves the conventional roads and steers down an entrance ramp to a special speedway with automated traffic lanes. Here, signal lights are controlled by a computer. Once on the speedway, the car is controlled by a computer system which regulates its speed and steering. Buried road cables send signals to electronic coils underneath the car. The driver is free to watch the morning television news and enjoy coffee and a Danish.

An alternate form of highly automated transportation is the pallet system. This is a sort of highway ferry. Vehicles drive onto platforms, each of which has its own power system. The platform is linked to an electronic guideway buried in the highway. Locking devices snap the car securely in place and the pallet moves off. Its course is controlled by the guideway until it reaches its selected destination. One platform can carry a number of cars and can save the fuel each individual car would have used.

Also under development is a commuter transportation system controlled by computers. It operates with the push of a button or the insertion of a coded card. The commuter who does not care to use his or her car every morning, or any morning, pushes a computer button to summon a driverless Compucab. The Compucab travels on automated highways and delivers a group of passengers to different destinations.

Commuters or shoppers who prefer a less expensive way to travel might take a brief walk to the nearest public transit station. There they could use its computer to send for a miniautobus or trolley car. The vehicle turns off from the express track to pick up the passenger. It then returns to the express track until it approaches the passenger's destination, turns off again, and stops at the selected station.

Predictions of these and other wonders of the future were first made decades ago. With the passing years, doubters have said they knew all along it wouldn't happen. Computerized cars! Auto-

"Looking Sweet" on a Bicycle Seat

*"It won't be a stylish marriage,
I can't afford a carriage
But you'll look sweet on the seat
Of a bicycle built for two."*

In 1892, when those now-famous lines from a song first appeared, the craze for bicycling was at its height. Bikes of various designs had been available for years, but they were unstable and unsafe. (Tricycles like the one at the upper left were far less risky.) Two breakthroughs—the introduction of an improved safety bicycle by James Starley and the development of a pneumatic tire by John Dunlop—led to the widespread popularity of the bicycle.

The arrival of the automobile ended the era of the bicycle. But today, because of gasoline shortages and a desire for physical fitness, bikes are once again popular. In developing countries especially, they are the primary conveyances. (At left is a street scene in Peking, China.)

What next? Light superbikes like the low-slung Vector, below. Still in the experimental stage, it can reach a speed of 58 miles per hour on human power alone.

mated roadways! You might as well try to send a man to the moon! But great progress has already been made in urban transportation. And there is a strong push for further change. More and more urban areas, for example, are keeping out autos while developing new, more efficient ways to bring people in and transport them on city streets.

One promising means of urban transportation is the PeopleMover. Most of us know it in its most basic form as what amounts to a conveyor belt or

"moving sidewalk" for pedestrians. The problem has been that it moves slowly in order to let passengers get on and off safely. Recently, however, faster walkway systems have been developed in Switzerland, France, and the United States. They are expected to come into widespread use during the 1990s. These PeopleMovers, with brand names such as Speedway and Variflex, operate at different speeds. The pedestrian steps on when the belt is going slowly, about two miles an hour. The belt then speeds up to about seven or ten miles per hour and slows down again as the pedestrian gets off. Accelerating walkways that are enclosed and climate-conditioned will replace conventional passageways in shopping districts and transportation terminals.

Computers and robots will handle refueling at future service stations. At left below, the batteries of an electric car are recharged. At right is a car that uses both battery power and liquid fuels.

In a more advanced form, the PeopleMover uses cars instead of just a moving belt. It has become a horizontal elevator that may run for distances ranging from a few yards to ten or fifteen miles. Many new airports and other buildings with large amounts of pedestrian traffic already have vehicular PeopleMovers. An excellent example is the enclosed PeopleMover in the new air terminal in Orlando, Florida. This is a horizontal elevator that looks like a large conventional up-down elevator.

But when its doors open, the passenger steps into a seatless car. The car can carry up to thirty-two thousand people an hour between the departure gates and the main terminal, a distance of about six hundred yards.

Other slightly different but related types of PeopleMovers have long been in use at such entertainment centers as Disneyland and Walt Disney World. These may use open cars that run on guideways or they may be streamlined, high-flying monorail trains *(see Glossary, Monorail).*

Besides PeopleMovers, there are now a number of new urban transportation systems that run on automatic controls. These systems are being used to connect areas within a city or between two nearby cities. Some of them may seem highly futuristic, but they are already in widespread use.

There are basically three varieties of what is commonly known as the AGT, or Automated Guideway Transit System. The simplest is the SLT, Single Line or Shuttle Loop Transit. It operates with large vehicles carrying large groups of passengers. The vehicles travel back and forth between two main stations, either on a single track or on a loop. They may make several stops or no stops at all, depending on the length of the run.

Somewhat more advanced is the GRT, or Group Rapid Transit System. This has a larger network of tracks than the SLT lines and uses slightly smaller vehicles that carry from six to fifty passengers each.

The third kind is the PRT, or Personal Rapid Transit System. It can provide an entire community with something close to individualized service. Two- to six-passenger cars run at timed intervals. The cars operate under computer control or on

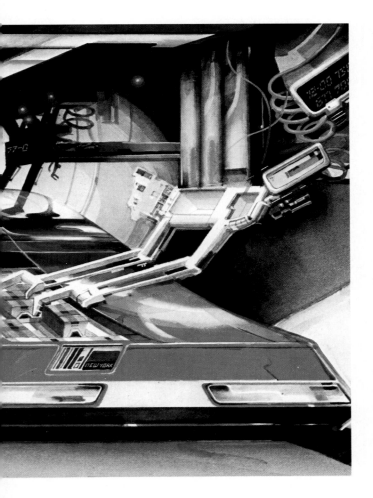

OVERLEAF: Highways of the future will be completely computerized. In this scene, an elevated, fast-lane artery, banked at corners and lit at the sides, sweeps large passenger cars and trucks along a fully automated speedway. Buried road cables transmit steering and speed instructions to the vehicles' computers. A local highway, also computer-controlled, passes under the fast lanes, carrying buses and small cars to the city in the distance. Alongside, an enclosed cycleway protects bike riders from the elements, as well as from other traffic. At lower right a speedy monorail waits for passengers at the station and computerized taxis, summoned by the touch of a button, stand ready for customers.

demand by passengers at the stations. To use a PRT system, the passenger first specifies the trip's origin and destination. Usually this is done by pushing buttons to enter these facts into the control system. A car is then summoned automatically. The car takes the user to the destination nonstop. To keep the system running without slowdowns, passengers get on and off on a side track so as not to obstruct the main line.

Various types of AGT systems are operating in many locations throughout the world. Many are at resorts. Others are in places such as Morgantown, West Virginia, Erlangen, West Germany, and at Duke University Hospital in Durham, North Carolina.

There are differences in the way these systems operate in different parts of the world. They may have small, open cars, linked together and moving continuously on an endless belt. They may have hundred-passenger vehicles that skim along on elevated guideways. They may use boxlike cable-cars suspended from overhead tracks. They may be designed in an amazing variety of other forms, whether monorail or tunnel train. The philosophy behind them all is the same: keep the system away from road traffic, preferably above or beneath street level, and make them as automatic as possible.

Comeback of the Railroad

Brother, have you seen the starlight on the rails?
Have you heard the thunder of the fast express?

Not lately, most Americans would reply to novelist Thomas Wolfe. And the same goes for many people around the world. There was a time when over sixty thousand locomotives linked the towns of the United States together. One billion passengers a year bought tickets to travel the rails. Every five seconds a train pulled out of a station somewhere in America.

Magical names like Le Train Bleu, the Orient Express, and the Flying Scotsman still linger in memory. Yet the truly great example of the thundering giants of the tracks ran in America. It was the elegant Twentieth Century Limited, which made its first New York–Chicago run on June 15,

1902. To serve twenty-seven passengers, the Century hauled three Pullman sleeping cars, a diner, a buffet, and a barber shop. It also carried a number of special crew members, including several maids and a stenographer. Running time for the trip was a maximum of twenty hours—thus the name "limited."

One English newsman was inspired to write: "Surely it is only an experiment! Can so high a rate of speed be maintained daily without injury to the engine?" Yes, it could. By 1938 the Century cut the trip to sixteen hours.

But after World War II, that sixteen hours seemed a lot. Highway transport, in the form of buses and trucks as well as automobiles, was cheaper, often more convenient, and almost as fast. Airplanes were much faster.

By the 1960s not only the Twentieth Century but almost all of the magnificent trains in the world were on their way out. For long-distance travel, the railroad seemed to be the wave of the past.

Yet the tracks remain. Total world trackage is about 750,000 miles. It is concentrated in countries such as the United States, Canada, the Soviet Union, India, and Australia, where vast distances invited the spread of the rail. This is an enormous resource, too important to waste.

Goods, far more than people, will continue to be moved in increasing quantities by workhorse railroad trains. Mainly, trains carry goods too heavy to be transported by air. They carry bulk goods of many kinds, such as grain, coal, and other ores that can be transported in enormous containers on flatcars. They carry vehicles that can be transported in three-decker auto conveyors.

The likelihood is that future freight trains will use the same fuel as the first locomotives—coal. But this coal will be burned in a high-speed, super-clean, high-energy furnace, which superheats the boiler to raise steam, which powers an electric generator, which in turn produces the electricity to run the train.

Meanwhile, railroad freight service is becoming more rapid and efficient than ever before. These days, nearly every operation is computerized, from maintaining the track to driving the train to locating and unloading individual shipments.

At the same time, the passenger train has been undergoing a change. It has been reborn in a number of forms as, essentially, a high-speed PeopleMover. The world may never see a glamorous Twenty-first Century Limited on rails, but new high-speed passenger trains now cut medium-

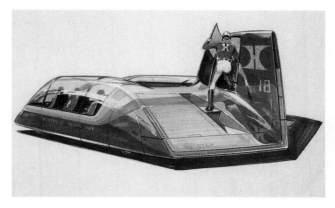

The operator of the multi-passenger tour bus above has a clear view from his elevated position at the rear.

Now under construction, Detroit's Downtown PeopleMover (below) features driverless cars traveling on an elevated guideway, above the traffic and pedestrians. The electrically powered cars, which will move at an average speed of 12.6 miles per hour, are expected to transport some seventeen million people annually along a 2.9-mile loop by 1990.

Congestion in large cities made the construction of mass transportation systems essential. The first underground subway was opened in London in 1863; because it was steam-operated, smoke was a problem in the tunnels. Today's electrically powered London subway, the world's largest, covers 158 miles on and under the ground. The New York City subway, opened in 1904, had some cars set aside exclusively for women, as the photo above shows.

distance trips of several hundred miles down to intercity express runs of close to airplane speed. Trains of this kind are already in service in many countries.

Railroaders looking for a way to speed up travel and bring back passenger traffic first asked: can new trains run an old tracks? The main problem was that many major routes had been built with a considerable number of curves. These required trains to slow down while rounding them—not so much to stay on the tracks as to avoid slamming passengers against or through the windows. If existing track was to be used, trains would have to be equipped with a tilt mechanism. This would

permit them to go around the high-speed curves by banking into a turn as an airplane does.

British Rail set out to solve this problem. At one point, after a discouraging test period, it almost gave up. But finally, British Rail developed its APT, or Advanced Passenger Train *(see Glossary).* The APT uses a system of jacks that tilts the carriages automatically on their bogies, or wheel units, as they travel around a curve. The tilting action is so effective that passengers are unaware that the train is taking a high-speed turn. The cars are lightweight, electrically powered, and equipped with advanced, high-powered brakes. The APT has been tested at 140 to 150 miles per hour. It is expected to carry passengers from London to the heart of Manchester or Liverpool or Glasgow in less time than an airplane flight would take.

An entirely different kind of train rocketed through Japan in 1964, the Shinkansen, popularly known as the Bullet Train *(see Glossary).* This train, which traveled on a specially built, nearly straight track between Tokyo and Osaka, hit speeds up to 125 miles per hour. At first, the Bullet Train chewed up its rails so badly that they were constantly in need of repair or replacement. But the system proved to be highly satisfactory. Several new lines were added and more are being developed. By 1980, test trains were achieving speeds of up to two hundred miles per hour. Operation is almost completely automated and absolutely accident-free.

The French Train à Grande Vitesse (TGV)—literally, High Speed Train—is at least as fast as the Japanese Bullet. Experimental French electric locomotives have been achieving speeds of over 150 miles per hour since 1954. In February 1981, the world speed record for conventional trains was shattered by a TGV trial run on the Paris-to-Lyon route, which reached 238 miles per hour. The route, officially inaugurated seven months later, consists of new track, almost all straight, and has no tunnels to slow the train down. Powered by twenty-five kilovolts of alternating current from overhead lines, powerful TGV locomotives develop up to eighty-five hundred horsepower. Each train has two power units, one at each end. There are eight passenger cars, and the train is operated by a single motorman. The top speed is two hundred miles per hour, but the need to conserve energy keeps it down to about 165. Before the TGV, the Paris-Lyon run took about four hours. Now it takes two hours flat.

The next new train to come down the rails is the Maglev, short for magnetic levitation. This train was developed some years ago at M.I.T. Never put to practical use in the United States, it is currently under development and being tested in West Germany and Japan.

The Maglev is a completely silent train that floats inches above the tracks on a cushion of air. The air cushion is created by powerful electromagnets in the train and in the track. The force of the magnets pushes the Maglev off the tracks.

Washington D.C.'s Metrorail, one of the newest mass transit systems (below), has been widely praised for the excellence of its architectural design.

Magnetic force also moves the train forward. Because there is no track friction to slow it down, the Maglev can reach very high speeds.

The West German Maglev has been tested successfully on a twenty-mile elevated track between Lathen and Doeroen in northern Germany. It zips along at two hundred miles per hour. Japanese Maglev trains, meanwhile, have achieved speeds in excess of 320 miles per hour. The Japanese Maglev system will almost surely be in operation on the Tokyo-to-Osaka run by 1990. It will beat the speedy Bullet Train's time of three and a half hours by a full two and a half hours.

Both the Bullet Train and the Maglev are under consideration for service in the United States. By 1988, a proposed California Bullet Train may link Los Angeles to San Diego in the time of fifty-nine minutes. It will be electrically powered and run on special tracks and prestressed ties. As for the Maglev, a 250-mph system could be in operation between Los Angeles and Las Vegas by mid-1991.

The Aérotrain, above, an experimental French train, operated like a hovercraft: eight blowers raised it off its track. The model above had a turboprop engine on top. The computer-driven California High Speed train below, expected to be operative by 1988, will travel at speeds up to 160 miles per hour.

These railroad advances are surpassed by the Planetran Express, a superfast train being developed by the Rand Corporation and other scientists. The Planetran is an ultra high-speed train that may introduce long-distance underground travel. One great benefit: there would be no need to tear up or change old tracks. The Planetran would rocket silently through the earth beneath us and connect with undersea routes.

By the year 2020, there could be a subway system extending from New York to Los Angeles, with supersonic missile shapes speeding through continent-long tubes or tunnels. The tunnels would be almost totally free of air, thus keeping air resistance to a minimum. Magnetically levitated above its tracks, the Planetran would flash through the semivacuum tunnel at fourteen thousand miles

per hour—much faster than supersonic speed. It would deposit its passengers in Los Angeles twenty-one minutes after leaving New York. Nonstop, that is: the local would take longer.

Building the Planetran could cost hundreds of billions of dollars. But operating costs would be low. And the train's other advantages are great: no air resistance, no track friction, no heat, no burning of fossil fuels, no pollution, and no tearing up of the countryside.

The tunnel required for such a project demands a massive digging job and a new way of digging. An appropriate tunneling device is available. Called the Subterrene, it was developed at the Los Alamos Scientific Laboratory in New Mexico. The drilling machine bores through rock at an incredible rate of speed. It melts the rock in the process, and as the molten rock cools the machine leaves behind it a smoothly glazed tunnel.

A Tunnel Ride Across the Country

All this leads to a vision of travel in the year 2020.

We descend on a high-speed walkway in an airlock tube to the Planetran station on the lower tip of Manhattan island. In the bright steel and marble station, a Planetran waits to depart on the Los Angeles run. At precisely 2:14 P.M., its computer-controlled doors slide silently together. The train departs, flashing forward as effortlessly as a fast-moving stream. Twenty-one minutes later, it glides into the Los Angeles station.

We leave the Planetran via an airlock system, step onto the walkway and arrive at the autocab stand. Entering a low-slung, driverless taxi, we tell its computer where we want to go. Our instructions show up on its screen, and the taxi angles onto the belt freeway that encircles Los Angeles. Seven minutes later, as we near our destination, the taxi moves to the outer lane. Its computer switches to the off-expressway control system and it drives off at the exit we want.

Almost like a car of today, it maneuvers through local streets and pulls into the driveway of our house. As we put our key in the door, the autocab silently zooms off to return to the cab rank, untipped but not unhappy.

The Disappearing Wheel

An economist who specializes in transportation, Wilfred Owen has had a longtime association with the prestigious Brookings Institution, a nonprofit research organization in Washington, D.C. He has served as a transportation consultant for various organizations, including the U.N. and the World Bank, and the countries of Japan, Brazil, and India. In the course of his work, he has traveled widely to observe and analyze transportation systems and developments in many parts of the world. He is the author of numerous articles and books on transportation, including The Accessible City. *In this interview, he talks about future developments in transportation.*

Q. Do you foresee great changes coming in transportation?
A. Yes. Look at the pace of change since 1900. It's amazing to realize that in 1900, the average American traveled about four hundred miles per year. Today that figure is up to twelve thousand. This century began with the horse and carriage, but soon it will be possible for ordinary citizens to travel in space. That means we'll be traveling a lot more miles.

Q. Do you see some overall trend developing as a guide to the changes coming in transportation?
A. Well, one way to answer that is to consider that after seven thousand years, we may be moving away from using the wheel as the basis for movement. The wheel is already disappearing in many aspects of the transportation of passengers and freight. I've felt for a long time that the day would have to come when the automobile would simply get off the ground. That's already happening to railroads with the magnetically levitated train. If the same thing happened with automobiles, you'd have cars traveling about the ground on guideways, a safe and speedy alternative to present highway travel. The possibilities for essentially wheel-less vehicles are strong. You could, for example, have a vehicle that lifted off the ground and supported itself on air jets, a form of transportation you now have with the hovercraft. This type of "flying car" might go along the ground for a short distances, but take off and travel a few feet in the air for long distances.

Q. Are there other signs that the wheel may be disappearing?
A. Well, wings take the place of wheels in aviation for all but the takeoff and landing. Even this limited use of the wheel is becoming less important. You now have helicopters and STOLs, planes that take off straight up from the ground or that rise and land at a sharp angle. They don't need much runway, and they may not need wheels. On the ground, we already have wheel-less belt conveyors and PeopleMovers. Pipelines are moving great volumes of oil and gas, and some countries are shipping bulk goods such as coal, chemicals, and ore through automated underground pipelines.

Q. What about the automated automobile? Is that going to happen?
A. It will take quite a while, but I believe it will happen. At that point, you would have automobiles traveling down electronically controlled guideways with their speed and braking also electronically controlled.

Q. What's preventing it from happening?
A. For one thing, there's the problem of controlling the spacing of vehicles on the guideway and the technical problem of controlling their side-to-side motion.

The computer is already playing a large role in the automobile engine, and we have to assume it will be used even more. Probably we can look for an early application of computers that guide drivers to destinations by means of controls that warn the drivers of problems at intersections and radar devices that control braking when cars get too close.

I believe the future of the completely automated automobile may be based on the electric car. With an electric car, you would draw power from cables in the highway. Drivers and batteries would be relied on to operate on local and secondary roads. On major highways, the computer would take over.

Q. What about automation in air travel?
A. Fully automated travel will obviously come first in planes. By 1990, the U.S. should have really modern air navigation and a microwave system that provides automatic landing. The new technology will make it possible to reduce traffic delays, avoid collisions, and use all of the air space available, instead of just flying "highways" in the sky as is the case now.

Q. Besides everything we've talked about, do you think some great breakthrough will come from what might be called an amateur inventor, a person fooling around with a great idea in his basement or attic?
A. It's entirely possible that an unexpected invention will come to us in that way. A rocket pack we can strap on our back that lets us go wherever we want, for instance. The big laboratories with lots of staff have taken over, but let's not forget what happened in the past. The Wright brothers are a wonderful example.

CHAPTER 5

The Future at Sea

It is said of many things that the world will never see their like again. But few objects of the past arouse fonder memories than the ocean giants whose day in the sun lasted less than half a century. The *Mauretania;* the *Aquitania;* the *Normandie;* the two *Queens, Mary* and *Elizabeth;* the *Ile de France*—these luxury liners were incomparable seagoing palaces.

It was not just the luxury and elegance of life on board that made them special—the silver-and-crystal dining rooms, the swimming pools, the gardens, the shops, the steam baths, the dog races, fancy dress balls, and flowing champagne. Equally important was the sense of adventure and romance, of heightened pleasure and a once-in-a-lifetime fling—as in a fairy tale, a Hollywood fantasy, a dream come true.

By the late 1960s, it was very nearly all gone, the great ships and the frantic fun. Passengers and crews alike mourned the passing of an era—passengers for the loss of luxury and glamor, crews for their love of sailing these giants across the seas.

Streamlined cruise ships are now considerably scaled down from the great ones. But they are still splendid and they still glide their way across the Atlantic and through warm vacation seas.

Today, airliners are faster and cheaper than surface ships and the most obvious and practical way to cross the oceans. But for those who love the sea they are an unworthy substitute.

Yet the future offers another option that may intrigue the most blasé of airline customers. Tomorrow's oceangoing craft may well be a train!

Boat trains have been in existence for as long as railroads. Trains arrive at the docks with passengers who then board ferries to cross a body of water. Depending on the body, some crossings can be rough. But in the best of future worlds, there is no need for them to be.

The hydrofoil at left, used to ferry commuters in Japan, can achieve speeds up to 50 miles per hour.

A new kind of land-sea link has now been forged with the completion of the underwater section of a railroad tunnel beneath Japan's Tsugaru Strait. The 33.7-mile tunnel links the main Japanese islands of Honshu and Hokkaido. Why such a tunnel? Because traffic between the islands is brisk and never-ending. The seas of the strait are so rough that surface travel is extremely dangerous. These treacherous seas have now been tamed by engineers burrowing beneath them. The rails have yet to be laid, but the completion date for a double track line is 1986.

The 33.7-mile length of the tunnel is not a vast distance. Yet, by the time the trains are functioning, the Tsugaru tunnel project will have taken fifteen years in the making. Completion after so many years of pioneering labor will be a milestone event. For the first time ever, a Bullet Train will shoot over tracks that are nearly all underwater.

And if it proves practical and cost-effective, the Japanese seatrain project may trigger others far more elaborate.

Tunnels like this one in other parts of the world are already being talked about. One is a shortcut under the English Channel from continental Europe to London and then to Edinburgh. An additional line would also pass under the Irish Sea to Dublin. An undersea tunnel from Italy to Sicily is another long-term possibility.

Looking even farther ahead, we can imagine someday traveling through railroad tubes suspended in the water and reaching from island to island and continent to continent. The first such

Symbolizing the glamorous era of luxury transatlantic crossings, the *Norway*, refurbished for Caribbean cruise duty, enters New York harbor in 1980.

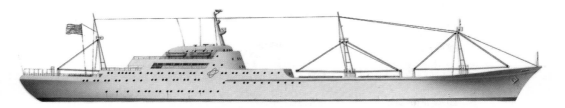

railroad tube may link Japan and South Korea via the Pusan Straits, a distance of one hundred miles.

We may yet see a high-speed, sea-land Bullet Train service that originates in Tokyo, crosses Asia and Europe before pausing in Paris, then rockets beneath the English Channel and proceeds to Ireland or Scotland. After that: North America, via an under-the-Atlantic Planetran.

The tunnel under the English Channel is an old, old dream that has never died. Some years after World War II, a Channel Tunnel Study Group was formed in England to plan the construction of what became known as the "Chunnel." In 1980 the British and French railroads agreed upon a basic tube design. It will initially accommodate seventy trains a day or about six million passengers a year, plus freight. Barring any more holdups, the Chunnel may be open for business before the year 2000.

New Forms of Sea Transportation

There will always be people who refuse to fly or to be whisked through underwater tubes and who prefer instead to sail across the oceans in passenger liners. And there will always be those who regard a leisurely ocean cruise as the ideal vacation. Traditional surface craft carrying passengers across the seas will be with us for years to come. But they will operate on a reduced scale and they will take a back seat to newer forms of sea transportation. Recycled medium-size passenger vessels and even conventional sailing ships will find new life. They will be used in the developing ports of the world as passenger carriers and to haul small cargoes. In more developed areas, the vast bulk of passenger traffic will be carried by airlines in the immediate future—until high-speed hovercraft and higher-speed tunnel trains take over.

Currently, the shipping industry is in a period of transition. It has been in an economic slump for the past ten years. It faces the challenge of dealing successfully with the related problems of cost, speed, and energy. Ships are slow and expensive to operate with presently available fuels.

One alternative power source is nuclear energy. For many years nuclear energy has been used on a limited basis by government agencies (not by

The United States government launched a nuclear cargo ship, *Savannah*, in 1959 as a demonstration of the peaceful uses of atomic energy.

shipping concerns) to propel icebreakers and submarines. The great advantage of nuclear-powered craft is the enormous range of ocean they can travel without refueling. But the costs of operating them are quite high, and public acceptance of nuclear power is less than enthusiastic. For these reasons, nuclear power is not an option for the immediate future of passenger vessels.

But finding an alternative energy source would not solve the industry's problems. Conventional ships cannot travel fast without burning up enormous quantities of fuel. They must overcome not only the air resistance encountered by all surface and aircraft, but also the even stronger drag or resistance created by the water *(see Glossary, Resistance)*. Whatever the power pushing the ship, this resistance reduces that power greatly. For a ship to move at a good speed it either has to push its engines to the utmost or get as much of its hull out of the water as possible without becoming airborne. If it were to become airborne it would no longer be a ship—at least not an ordinary one.

Neither the hydrofoil nor the hovercraft is an ordinary ship. Each one almost flies.

The first hydrofoil vessel was built in 1905 by an Italian engineer and airship designer named Enrico Forlanini *(see Glossary, Hydrofoil)*. The lifting device from which the vessel gets its name is similar to the wing or rudder of a plane. But the hydrofoil develops lift as it passes through water instead of air. The foils it travels on are wings of a sort, but they are more finlike than winglike. These foils are attached to struts on either side of the vessel. As the craft gains speed, they lift the hull clear out of the water, leaving little more than the propeller submerged. In this way, the drag ordinarily caused by the vessel's contact with the water is reduced considerably.

In 1911, Forlanini demonstrated the latest of his series of improved hydrofoil models to American inventor Alexander Graham Bell, who was then visiting Lake Maggiore in Italy.

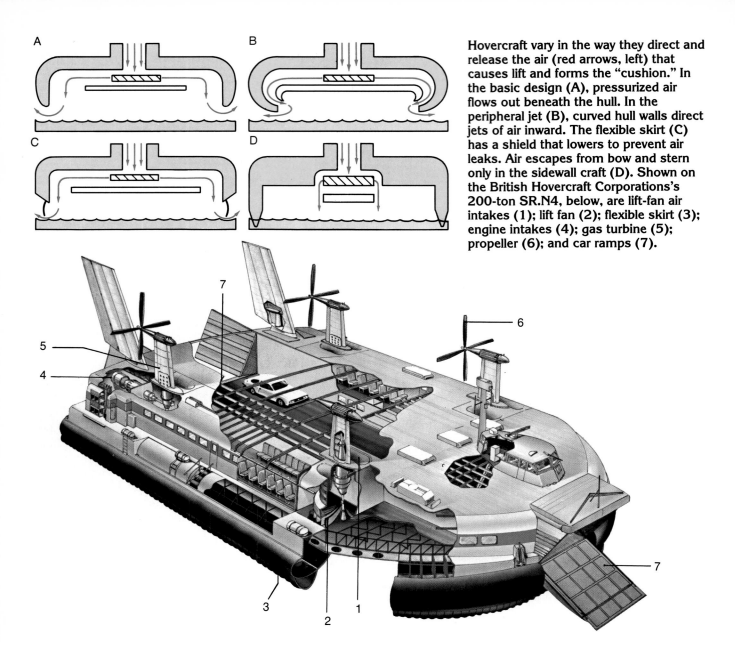

Hovercraft vary in the way they direct and release the air (red arrows, left) that causes lift and forms the "cushion." In the basic design (A), pressurized air flows out beneath the hull. In the peripheral jet (B), curved hull walls direct jets of air inward. The flexible skirt (C) has a shield that lowers to prevent air leaks. Air escapes from bow and stern only in the sidewall craft (D). Shown on the British Hovercraft Corporations's 200-ton SR.N4, below, are lift-fan air intakes (1); lift fan (2); flexible skirt (3); engine intakes (4); gas turbine (5); propeller (6); and car ramps (7).

Bell was interested in anything pertaining to aviation. He was intrigued by the hydrofoil concept and proceeded to develop his own version of the skimmer craft. In 1918, Bell's HD-4 achieved a top speed of 70.86 miles per hour.

That test speed, then a record, is easily achieved today. Hydrofoils, along with speedboats and waterskis, are among the fastest things to move over the waves.

Hydrofoils have one drawback. They are vulnerable to floating wreckage and heavy seas. But this has not stopped their use as fast-moving passenger ferries and commuter craft in such widely scattered areas as the coastal waters of Norway, the Black Sea, the Adriatic, and the Thames River in England. At least nine hundred hydrofoils are now operating in Eastern Europe.

Experts predict that future hydrofoils will have sensors that detect high waves and bobbing objects and signal the foils to rise above them. These improved hydrofoils will be used more and more throughout the world in the coming decades. A much larger version will also probably be developed to serve as luxurious floating hotels of the future. These fast-moving hotels will be able to "park" anywhere on the ocean or in any harbor.

Even more versatile than the hydrofoil is the hovercraft. Faster than the hydrofoil, the hovercraft is even more like an aircraft than its sister ship. It's a kind of amphibian that can float across either land or sea, so long as the surface is relatively smooth. The bigger the hovercraft is, the higher it can rise. And the higher it can rise, the less it is obstructed by surface obstacles.

The possibilities of such a craft were first examined by British radio engineer Christopher Cockerell. Cockerell became a boatbuilder after World War II. He found that what he called skin and wave resistance greatly diminished the performance of his boats. He determined to find a way to reduce friction against the hulls of his craft. He theorized that if he could make the skin of a boat "a skin of air," then he could almost eliminate friction.

What ultimately evolved was a kind of flying boat, variously labeled Hovercraft, Levjet, or Air Cushion Vehicle (ACV). There are several forms of this vessel, under different names. Probably the most familiar is the one supported by a four-foot cushion of pressurized air created by the downward blast of one or more fans built into the hull.

The advantages of this craft are many. Capable of skimming directly from the water up a concrete ramp or a sandy beach, it needs no dock or airfield. Its power requirements are much less than those of helicopters or seaplanes of the same weight. Its speed—in some cases, more than one hundred miles per hour—is higher than that of other surface ships and most land vehicles. And it seems likely that it can be built to almost any size, bigger even than the largest conventional passenger liners or freighters.

The ACV, in fact, has a solid future as a cargo carrier. A great deal of heavy freight can only be transported by sea. In the immediate future, the great bulk of sea travel will be devoted to the hauling of freight. Many once-busy passenger ports are now deserted, their clientele having transferred their allegiance to airports. But some of these ports will find new prosperity in the future as cargo centers. And the chances are excellent that some of the cargo carriers will be ACVs. Cushion ships of several thousand tons are already under development. Large hovercraft are now being used to ferry cars across the English Channel. The more optimistic forecasters predict that 10,000-ton nuclear-powered hovercraft freighters could soon be traveling over deeper seas and longer distances.

The possibility of using gigantic hovercraft to haul heavy loads of sea freight has suggested an even bolder engineering dream. This would use the air-cushion craft in an ingenious scheme of portage, the practice of hauling boats and supplies overland between navigable waters. Greeks of ancient times used to transport their boats across the Isthmus of Corinth on oxcarts. Indians of North America carried canoes on their backs from river to lake to river. Small marine railways or railway canals have for centuries been used in Europe to move ships from one waterway to another. In terms of the technology required, there seems no reason why a cargo ship from one ocean or inland waterway could not be carried across country on the back of an ACV to some other ocean or canal.

Some engineers have even grander schemes for moving seagoing vessels between seas. One option is a bigger and better railroad. It would have trains with enormous cars that could carry ships across the land. Another is a highway upon which gigantic trucks would carry ships piggyback, like containers on a flatbed.

Great freight barges that are more conventional but still impressive already travel on rivers, canals, and intercoastal waterways. The Eurobarge, for example, is able to carry a thousand tons of cargo and is widely used in the inland waters of Europe.

For the immediate future, the improvement in inland-ocean connections lies in an increasing use of containers. The goal is to turn freight movement into a continuous process, so that freight can travel on rail, highway, river, canal, and sea. Containers make this possible, and containerization is already well under way in the more developed countries of the world.

There is one other simple and efficient way to smooth the flow of various forms of water traffic. That is to piggyback inland vessels, complete with their loads, onto oceangoing ships. The ships then transport the piggybacked vessels with their cargo to a distant port. They unload them where inland waters meet the sea, so that the inland ships can resume their journey on inland waters.

A somewhat different plan is based on the idea that such piggybacking might not always be practical. This would be the case where coastal ports were too shallow to accommodate oceangoing vessels. The plan is to make the harbor suitable for oceangoing ships by constructing offshore

The three-wheeled Darter, above, is a land/sea vehicle that would be powered by water jets while afloat. Below is an offshore air terminal, built on a man-made island. Because the terminal would be situated 20 to 30 miles offshore, noise from the aircraft would not be bothersome. Fuel for the planes might someday be provided by hydrogen from the sea.

port facilities. These facilities would permit the transfer of cargoes of any type from deep-water ships to shallow-draft vessels.

Floating Cities on the Seas

This idea leads directly to visions of artificial islands, which would be created to fulfill a variety of needs. Such islands are now mostly in the think-tank or drawing-board stage. But some have already been built.

At the Japanese port of Kobe, for instance, Japanese engineers have constructed stepping-stone islands to provide convenient access to their off-shore coal mines. Fulfilling a similar purpose are the offshore oil-drilling platforms of the North Sea and the Pacific. In the near future, we are likely to see much greater use of such anchored or movable sea platforms. The possibilities are boundless. Among the facilities that would be built on

such platforms are nuclear power plants, oil refineries, steel mills, waste-disposal plants, public utilities of all kinds, and major industrial complexes. Floating out in the open sea, these huge, stable platforms could minimize dangers from accidents and pollution.

The idea of the aircraft carrier—minus its military function—might well be expanded into an entire airport facility located several miles offshore. The floating airport would be composed of units fastened together, and it could be endlessly extended with the addition of other such units. The airport thus could be as large as required to accommodate increasing traffic, without increasing noise and pollution in nearby residential areas.

There could be residential areas on the water, too, floating off heavily populated coasts and far from the power plants and airports. As available land shrinks and the price of real estate soars, it becomes more and more likely that the sea will be exploited for personal as well as public purposes.

Some futurists are already seriously entertaining the notion of constructing a sea city, capable of accommodating thirty thousand people, off the coast of Norfolk, England. The hydrofoil would probably be the vehicle of choice to link the mainland with artificial islands such as this until—and probably even after—submarine tunnels are built.

The technology exists to undertake these projects right now. But the enormous costs and the inevitable disagreements among the many interests likely to be involved pose problems that probably will not be solved in the near future.

Computerized Cargo Handling

Meanwhile, our freight-carrying ships will get bigger as their crews get smaller. Superships already transport enormous quantities of bulk and container goods, such as oil, grain, ores, industrial equipment, machine parts, and major household appliances. The modern supertankers that ferry oil from the Middle East to the West are among the largest man-made structures in the world: the biggest are 1,150 feet long, almost 500,000 tons in weight, and have decks the size of a hundred tennis courts. Future versions of these titans may be nuclear-powered, oil-fired, or even coal-driven. If

The huge hovercraft above, seen at EPCOT's World of Motion, is a floating hotel. It could move between ports on a cushion of air at 50 miles per hour.

they use coal, special furnaces will burn the coal cleanly and with a minimum of waste.

Future cargo ships may have sails as well as engines to supplement their main power plants. Some already do. The sails are not the wonderful billowing canvas of old, but instead large rigid panels controlled by computers to make maximum use of the wind. These sail-driven ships will have new sail forms made of new materials. They will receive weather information supplied by satel-

OVERLEAF: Seaports of tomorrow are likely to be bustling, multi-use centers of activity—a far cry from today's underdeveloped facilities where all too often rotting piers lie abandoned. At this gleaming harbor, a waiting hovercraft (lower right) takes on vehicles as well as passengers who have arrived at the adjacent terminal via bullet trains. Huge, floating container barges (center), guided by tugs, leave their mother ship and approach the docks (left), where they are off-loaded by gigantic robot "longshoremen." Also berthed at the wharf are a sleek ocean liner, private yachts, and hydrofoils that ferry residents to a floating sea city (upper right). Just offshore (center right), a cargo submarine surfaces preparatory to disgorging its fleet of freight-loaded vessels. A solar-powered yacht and other fun craft sail between the hovercraft and the cargo submarine. Overhead, a low-flying airship cruises by.

lite. They will employ computerized operating systems to dictate the precise set of the sails. All these elements will combine to make wind-aided vessels far more efficient than they ever were in the past.

Future cargo ships will deliver their freight to docks equipped with advanced unloading equipment. Robot vehicles and robot handlers will manipulate much of the cargo according to instructions given by computers functioning as foremen. The human touch will finally be phased out of the essentially mechanical business of freight handling. In a further move toward electronic control, unpowered yet floatable freight containers will be loaded into colossal powered vessels that will convey them across the sea. They will be unloaded in distant harbors, where they will be docked or maneuvered inland by electronic or other automated systems. The mother ships themselves will be manned by minimal crews or altogether automated. They will be guided by onboard computers receiving navigation and other instructions from satellites in orbit overhead.

At an even later date, nuclear power will become a controlled, readily available, and completely acceptable source of driving energy. Submersible nuclear freighters will then be able to dip under the surface of storm-tossed seas and travel smoothly in the calm beneath. Predictions are for giant-size submarine-carrier freighters that can accommodate a flock of smaller freight subs in their cargo bay. The smaller subs will carry container freight and will be capable of operating independently of the mother ship. Both the larger and the smaller subs will be controlled by computers.

Near the destination port, the mammoth mother sub will surface offshore and open its massive cargo doors. The smaller subs, preprogrammed, will slip into the water and glide into port. The usual work gang of robots at the automated docks will then proceed with the unloading. While this is going on, other container subs will cruise out to the carrier ship.

The submarine vessels of the future will be capable of high-speed travel down in the quiet depths. These submarines are not likely to appeal to long-distance passengers, even if they are available for passenger use.

New Worlds Under the Sea

But for short distances, submarines may play a leading role in sea transportation. We are becoming ever more conscious of the rich resources of the sea and our own dwindling living space. We may find that underwater living stations offer as much promise as floating city islands. There is a vast expanse of unexplored, unused territory below. It offers tremendous potential for farms and homes of a type now barely imaginable.

Almost certainly, the first permanent underwater living places will be experimental stations, consisting of observation posts, laboratories, and small farms. They would be manned by scientific specialists of various kinds. Comforts would be minimal: pioneers seldom have much fun.

Later, undersea cities will be built. The first of these may be created by the necessity to escape the crowded earth. It will be a carefully designed place containing all of the facilities, and more, that are available topside. The weather would be controlled to offer variety to underwater citizens and to aid the growth of domesticated crops and vegetation. And there would be the eternally changing underwater scenery to look out upon. The community, or habitat, would float in the sea's depths and be topped off with a surface superstructure accommodating an aircraft landing pad and docking facilities for surface craft.

Another community of underwater stations will exist at the deepest underwater level, on the ocean bottom. Here there will be facilities such as fish and plant farms. There will be storage areas for experimental equipment used to explore and tap the ocean floor. And there will be docks, airlocks, and service and maintenance facilities for underwater vessels. Small one- to four-person submarines will dart back and forth among these underwater installations, acting as messenger ships and taxis. They will surface at times to exchange passengers and mail packages with surface craft or island installations.

Within the coming century, many of us may be living on ocean islands or in underwater colonies. Life on or in the ocean will take us away from noise and fumes. Some of us will be harvesting the seas and mining the ocean floor. Others will

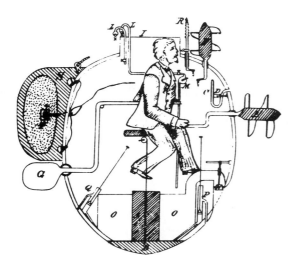

David Bushnell's wooden *Turtle*, above, tried unsuccessfully to sink a British ship in 1776. The 560-foot-long, nuclear-powered submarine *Ohio* (below) can carry 24 nuclear missiles with a 4,000-mile range.

The Nautilus Sails On

In 1870, Jules Verne described an elaborate submarine, the Nautilus, *in his book,* Twenty Thousand Leagues Under the Sea. *But attempts to create a real submarine up to that time were primitive at best. Robert Fulton's metal* Nautilus *of 1801 and the U.S. Navy's first submarine, the U.S.S.* Holland *of 1900, were forerunners of the diesel submarines used extensively in both world wars. Nuclear submarines that could stay submerged for many months date from the 1954 launch of still another* Nautilus. *In 1960 the nuclear ballistic missile submarines that now prowl the world's oceans came into use.*

be going to our schools or offices much as in ages past. As sea dwellers, we will become so much a part of the sea that it will be our major playground. All of us will have access to the little solar sailboats in the public marinas and to the family-size hydroplanes that whisk along above the water's surface. Athletic speedsters will do tricks on their motorized individual surfboards. Others will glide over

the sea highways on surfbikes or motorcycles with floats—sometimes called wetbikes or waterbuggies.

For quieter times, we will go off on vacations away from our underwater city. We may use small transparent subboats to tour distant coral reefs and sunken mountaintops and gaze at strange creatures of the deep even as they peer at us. And some of us may board solar-powered cruisers that take us on silent, leisurely trips up lakes and rivers to visit our friends on the continents where once we lived.

The cargo in this massive, computer-controlled submarine freighter is stored in smaller vessels that sail to the dock when the sub reaches its destination. Previously loaded vessels with other freight sail out to the sub, which submerges and heads for a new port.

CHAPTER 6

Flying Higher, Faster, and Farther

Every year, hundreds of millions of passengers fly the airlines of the world. They board scheduled flights on carefully maintained aircraft flown by highly trained pilots. Their journey is guided by a worldwide network of air traffic controllers and the latest in advanced electronic equipment. When they arrive, they walk into a terminal with all the facilities of a small city.

To most of us, it seems as if air travel has always been this way. But in the beginning, it was quite different.

The beginning was the year 1919, when Britain, France, Germany, and Switzerland each began an air passenger transport service. The planes were veterans of World War I, mostly fragile little biplanes with two-to-four seat enclosed cabins and an open cockpit for the pilot—a war veteran himself. A few of the larger converted bombers, such as the British Handley Page 0/400, seated as many as six or seven intrepid passengers, but scarcely in luxurious surroundings.

The first commercial transport companies came and went, often, it seemed, almost overnight. Still, under various names, several airlines very early began the regular operations that led to their position as giants in today's aviation industry. KLM of the Netherlands was one, Belgium's Sabena another, and BOAC of Britain a third. These pioneers found out what they were doing by doing it, and they blazed a trail for other companies and countries to follow.

Passengers on the fledgling airlines had few comforts. They flew in slightly modified wartime surplus craft. The guns and bomb racks had been removed, and the cabin had been refitted—if the passengers were lucky. There were no navigation aids, no air traffic controls, no radios. The water-

Shot by rockets to a suborbital trajectory beyond the atmosphere, hypersonic spaceplanes of the future will be able to fly from America to Japan in an hour.

81

cooled engines of the primitive planes were heavy, leaky, and a constant source of trouble. Airports consisted of wartime hangars, wooden storage shacks, and narrow, unpaved runways.

Change came slowly. Two-way radio was the first major improvement. Next came new airplanes, specially designed for civilian transport, built by Junkers in Germany, Fokker in the Netherlands, and de Havilland in England. Then came the big breakthrough: an improved air-cooled engine, much more efficient and much less prone to breakdown than the old radiator type still used in many planes at that time.

Food and other services followed. Food became even more important as the European airlines extended their long-distance routes to other continents with few aviation facilities of their own. A trip to Africa or South America, for example, might involve several days of tedious travel. Rest stops came in places that had no airports, to say nothing of restaurants or hotels. Planes landed on strips cleared by the airline companies themselves. They were serviced by the airlines' own personnel. Passengers and crews stopped over at rest houses provided by the airlines or at military bases.

The modified warplanes were soon replaced by planes designed specifically for the comfort and convenience of passengers. They had heated cabins, upholstered seats, service facilities, and slightly reduced engine noise and vibration. But even then, the fragility of the aircraft, their slow speeds, short range, and frequent refueling stops continued to be a problem.

Another long-lasting drawback was the lack of pressurization. To avoid the hazards of high altitude, planes had to maintain a cruising altitude of less than ten thousand feet. (Present-day aircraft maintain a cabin altitude, or pressure, of eight thousand feet.) Unfortunately, at low levels the planes were at the mercy of weather and turbulence. These factors sometimes resulted in considerable unpleasantness.

Still, up to the beginning of World War II, aircraft manufacturers made vast improvements in the safety and comfort features of their product. Biplanes gave way to the sleeker and more efficient monoplanes. Stress-tested metal replaced wood and fabric fuselages on planes that had a number of engines instead of just one. Navigational systems, instruments for "flying blind," automatic pilots, retractable wheels, and de-icing equipment became standard. Airports had concrete runways as well as facilities for both planes and people. Airline companies established a network of air routes and built it into a complex, far-flung system of transport. It was already obvious that air transportation would have a dramatic effect on our lives. Far faster than any other form of transportation, air travel was poised to change the way people conducted business and arranged their leisure time.

As destructive as World War II was, it produced positive results for air transport. The enormous technological advances made in the war years were reflected in a postwar boom in commercial flight. Aircraft manufacturers, particularly in America, learned a great deal in a hurry. They were also able to turn their wartime knowledge immediately to peacetime use. Less than a year after the war ended, the Boeing, Lockheed, and Douglas aircraft companies were ready with greatly improved passenger airliners.

Airline companies were no less ready to tap a new market with their new planes. So superbly fitted and luxurious were the postwar planes that it was almost possible for travelers to spend vacations on board. Airlines offered gifts of exotic flowers and expensive perfumes. They served multicourse meals and magnums of champagne. Planes had spacious lounges, dining areas, and even, on some long-distance flights, sleeping berths. All of these luxuries combined to fulfill the traveler's dream of airborne elegance.

The four-engine DC-6 Dayplane-Sleeper was a perfect example. Among its attractions were two lounges, a buffet area, a cloakroom, and fifty-two sumptuously padded seats which could be transformed into twenty-six sleeping berths. Rivaling

Pan Am's *China Clipper*, a Martin M-130, flies over the unfinished Golden Gate Bridge bound for the Philippines on her inaugural run in 1935.

this fine skyliner was the 70-ton Stratocruiser, a double-decked Boeing 377 descended from the World War II B-29 bomber. Capable of carrying many more passengers, the spacious Stratocruiser seated a mere sixty-one paying persons. But it gave them plenty of space to relax in a family travel compartment situated aft of the cockpit. On a lower level, it also had a midship bar-lounge reached by a spiral staircase. Fully pressurized, the big four-engine, split-level plane cruised at twenty-five thousand feet to avoid low-altitude bumps. Passengers could move about as much as they wanted. Full-course meals, including wine, were served on individual tables attached to the seats. Inaugurated in the mid-1940s, the Stratocruiser was the biggest, speediest airliner of its time.

Then along came the Connie, Lockheed's graceful triple-tailed 1649A Constellation. This fifty-six-passenger speedster could reach all the Western European capitals nonstop from New York. Beautifully designed, solidly engineered, superbly fitted, equipped with a roomy lounge and an observation port, the Connie seemed destined to become one of the world's favorite planes. TWA put the first of them into service in April 1957, and it was an instant hit.

But another trend was already in progress. No matter how attractive, the passenger airliners had shown that they were not the absolute answer to the ocean liners. Capacity was fine, comfort and luxury were fun, speed was picking up. But all of this was not quite enough to make passengers

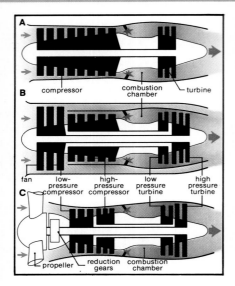

In the **turbojet** (diagram A above), first of the three basic jet engines, power comes from the escape of expanding gases. Air sucked into the front of the engines (blue) by compressors is forced back into a combustion chamber where it mixes with fuel. The burning mixture produces expanding gases (red) that blast out through the rear, thrusting the aircraft forward. The exhaust also spins a turbine that powers the compressors. **Turbofan** engines (B) have an extra turbine and a compressor-fan to divert part of the incoming air through ducts around the engine to provide extra thrust. A **turboprop** (C) contains a turbine-driven propeller to provide thrust.

These three engines are capable of speeds up to Mach 3. The **ramjet**, however, can achieve Mach 5. It has no moving parts, but rams or compresses sucked-in air by its speed alone. On the drawing boards is the Supersonic Combustion Ramjet—the **scramjet**—which would burn air and liquid oxygen in a supersonic combustion chamber and could achieve speeds up to Mach 15.

rave about the wonders of plane flight. For one thing, even the most superbly designed airplanes were still noisy. Piston-engined, propeller-driven, they roared and vibrated. No matter how cushy their cabins, the pounding power plants still disturbed travelers. For another, airline travel was very expensive. The high fares restricted air travel to a fortunate few. This was not what the airlines had had in mind when they expanded their markets and offered various lures to attract passengers. For all but urgent overseas trips, the mass of travelers still went by rail and road and even sea.

It was clear that a new approach was needed: less luxury for the few, more seats for the many, lower fares for all, more power for less weight, and higher speeds.

The solution was the jet: a different kind of aircraft. The jet replaced the piston-driven propeller system with the jet engine, a revolutionary new type of power plant (see Glossary, Internal Combustion Engine and Turbojet Engine). The jet burned a mixture of compressed air and fuel and exhausted a jet stream of gases to produce its forward thrust.

On May 2, 1952, a de Havilland Comet bearing the colors and logo of the British Overseas Airways Corporation (BOAC) took off from Heathrow Airport on its maiden flight to Johannesburg, South Africa. The world's first passenger jetliner, it was a sleek and beautiful bird that measured ninety-three feet from its propellerless nose to its tail. With two turbojet engines in each wing, the Comet had almost five times the power of the piston-engined DC-6. It was capable of flying almost five hundred miles an hour at thirty-five thousand feet—above turbulence and without vibration.

Up till then, the London to Johannesburg trip had taken forty hours. The Comet made five interim stops and arrived at its destination just twenty-three and a half hours after leaving home. It was a monumentally impressive flight and an enormous triumph. The jet age had arrived like a comet, or so it seemed.

For several months, the Comets flew their routes with similar success. Then the accidents began. Two occurred on takeoff, the second re-

A thundering sonic boom over the Mojave Desert on October 14, 1947 signaled the start of the jet age as test pilot Chuck Yeager rocketed through the sound barrier, reaching Mach 1.06—670 mph—in the Bell X-1, above. The swept-wing, 153-foot-long Boeing 707 passenger jetliner, left, had its first scheduled flight in 1958. It cruised at 590 mph. The 204-foot-long Anglo-French SST, *Concorde* (below), introduced in 1976, travels at 1,354 mph.

sulting in 100 percent fatalities. The third came during a violent thunderstorm: the plane disintegrated in flight in what was apparently a natural tragedy. The fourth happened while the plane was climbing routinely to its cruising altitude of thirty-six thousand feet. Without warning and in a clear sky, the plane came apart and its pieces fell flaming into the sea.

All Comets were immediately grounded and examined for possible clues to the cause of this disaster. The scattered remnants of the underwater wreck were fished up and examined. While this was going on, another Comet fell from the skies as it climbed to cruising altitude.

Investigative efforts were intensified. Fuselages and parts were subjected to exhaustive examinations. A grounded Comet was put through rigorous pressure tests in a specially built water tank. Finally, a diagnosis of the fatal flights could be made. Explosive decompression had resulted from a crack in the fuselage caused by premature metal fatigue. No airplane had ever before climbed so high and so fast. The specifications for the Comet had been rigorous, but no one had anticipated the great effect that pressurization stresses would have on the skin of the pioneer plane.

Comet 1 was laid to rest. To the doomsayers, it seemed that both the jet plane and the British aircraft industry had been dealt a fatal blow.

But the doomsayers were wrong on both counts.

The jet triumphed in the form of the BOAC Comet 4. Its fuselage, engines, and other components were so extensively modified that it represented a major redesign of the ill-fated Comet 1. The Comet 4 inaugurated the first lasting transatlantic jetliner service on October 4, 1958, flying between London and New York. It carried sixty-seven passengers and soon proved itself to be a safe and sturdy airplane.

Only twenty-two days later—October 26, 1958—a Paris-bound Pan American flight took off from New York's international airport to the sound of bands, the popping of corks, and politicians proclaiming the *real* arrival of the Jet Age. It was a historic occasion, the first scheduled flight of an American jetliner, a Boeing 707. The transatlantic service it inaugurated was to continue uninterrupted for a quarter of a century and more.

The tough-skinned, high-flying 707 carried 111 passengers and 11 crew members. It took eight hours and forty-one minutes to fly from New York to Paris, including a refueling stop at Gander,

Powered by solar cells and a small electric engine, California engineer Paul MacCready's delicate, dragonfly-like *Solar Challenger* flew across the English Channel in 1981 in 5 hours, 23 minutes.

Newfoundland. With its large passenger capacity and its cruising speed of 590 miles per hour, the 707 was a significant advance in air travel.

Still, it was a long way from being the fastest thing in the air.

Breaking the Sonic Barrier

Since the 1930s, the aviation community had been aware of something described as "the sound barrier." This unseen but formidable aerial obstacle was caused by shock waves forming around an airplane that traveled close to the speed of sound. The shock waves, it was said, would cause vibrations violent enough to rip a plane apart. In 1941, a high-speed Lockheed P-38 jet had slammed into the supposed barrier during a test flight and had dived screaming to the ground.

Thereafter, many aeronautical theoreticians convinced themselves that any aircraft approaching the speed of sound was doomed to go out of control. It would either shudder itself to pieces or drop like a meteorite. The sound barrier, they said, was impenetrable.

The sound or sonic "barrier" is actually a type of drag, or resistance. It is created by the aircraft itself as it moves through the air close to the speed of sound. That speed varies with the temperature and the plane's altitude. At sea level, it is about 760 miles per hour. At high altitude, where the temperature is lower—say, at forty thousand feet —it drops to about 660 miles per hour *(see Glossary, Supersonic Speed)*.

Airmen needed to arrive at some degree of precision in measuring, or at least describing, this speed. They began expressing sonic and supersonic speeds in terms of Mach numbers. The name honored a nineteenth-century Austrian physicist named Ernst Mach, who had studied and measured both the speed and properties of sound. In this system, an object traveling at the speed of sound—whether 760 miles per hour at sea level or 660 at higher altitude—is traveling at a velocity of Mach 1. At twice that speed, its velocity is Mach 2. At 80 percent of that speed, it is Mach 0.8.

Planes traveling in excess of Mach 0.7 were in danger of creating shock waves that could destroy them. Or such was the theory, and it seemed borne out during the war years when a series of high-speed fighters crashed after vibrations had ripped off their tails. Various modifications of tail surfaces, wings, and braking devices failed to correct what was clearly a major problem. This lent support to the pessimistic theory that there was indeed a barrier that could not safely be penetrated.

The challenge was to build a craft that could test that barrier by going through it. And this should be done not in a chance dive, as had occurred before, but by design and under control. Part of the solution would lie in the design of the test plane and part in its power plant. The jets of the early forties lacked the thrust to ram an aircraft through Mach 1. But aeronautical scientists sur-

Bert and Dick Rutan designed these sportplanes, which have wings mounted on the nose; the design increases the plane's ability to maneuver without stalling. Pilots buy the plans and parts and build the plane at home themselves.

mised that a powerful rocket engine might successfully propel a high-speed research aircraft at supersonic speed. The job of developing a rocket-powered test craft was undertaken by the Bell Aircraft Corporation of Buffalo, New York, for the Army Air Forces *(see Glossary, Rocket Engine).*

Developmental work began in December 1944. The aircraft as it emerged two years later was an exceptionally sturdily built thirty-one-foot winged rocket. It was designated as Experimental Sonic 1 but was known from the beginning as the X-1. It would be carried under the belly of a B-29 Superfortress and released at a height of more than twenty thousand feet. The site chosen for the flight tests was Rogers Dry Lake near Muroc Airfield in California's Mojave Desert.

During earlier tests, beginning in 1946 and continuing into the fall of 1947, the little plane performed superbly. But it did encounter shock waves and heavy buffeting as it reached speeds of Mach 0.8 and more. Two questions remained. Could the X-1 penetrate its own shock wave at Mach 1? And would the pilot be able to control the pitch of the plane as it did so?

The pilot was Charles E. "Chuck" Yeager, a twenty-four-year-old veteran of World War II. On the morning of the flight, October 14, 1947, Yeager climbed aboard the B-29 mother ship. He was silently suffering severe pain after being thrown by a bolting horse several days before. Minutes later, at five thousand feet, Yeager lowered himself into the cockpit of the X-1. Surveying the controls of the four-engine, needle-nose craft he had dubbed *Glamorous Glennis* (after his wife), he prepared for takeoff.

At twenty thousand feet above the dry lake bed, the pilot of the mother ship released the X-1 and Yeager triggered the test craft's rocket power. The small plane flashed skyward, climbing through thirty-seven thousand feet to forty-two thousand. Shock waves began to buffet it.

A sound as if from a bomb blast split the sky and reverberated across the desert. This was a sonic boom, signaling the piercing of the barrier. In perfect control of his craft, Yeager had thrust the X-1 through the "impossible" obstacle at slightly above Mach 1.

The X-1 was just the beginning. A series of supersonic X-craft followed, setting new speed and altitude records. Several test pilots went well beyond the top supersonic speed of Mach 5 into hypersonic speed *(see Glossary, Supersonic Speed).* In 1967, Major William Knight took the X-15A-2 to a height of almost one hundred thousand feet at a record speed of Mach 6.72—4,520 miles per hour. By the time the X-15 program ended in 1969, the altitude record had been raised to 354,200 feet—more than sixty-seven miles above the earth and almost into space.

Within a few years, supersonic passenger planes were in the air. They were not, however, American aircraft. Boeing's plans to develop a supersonic transport, or SST, were defeated by public opposition to the plane's high noise level. There was also a judgment that the SST would not produce profits large enough to justify the huge financial investment that the United States government would have to make. The SSTs that went into service in 1976 were Anglo-French Concordes, built in a unique collaboration between the governments of Britain and France. Delta-winged, bird-nosed, slim-lined, the Concordes cruised at Mach 2 and had a range of over three thousand miles. Passengers could keep track of the plane's speed by keeping an eye on the Machmeters mounted on the cabin walls.

Critics predicted that the Concorde would never be a success. They cited defects such as tiny windows, cramped seats, limited capacity—one hundred passengers, four abreast—and high ticket prices. Public complaints about the sonic

Current experimental aircraft, top to bottom above, include the NASA/Air Force HiMAT with winglets and canard wing; the NASA Ames/Dryden-1 (AD-1), whose oblique wing pivots from 0 to 60 degrees, and the helicopter-like X-wing with rotor blades that lock at high subsonic speeds.

Flying into the Future

And for those who prefer a sense of spaciousness, a cheaper seat, and more conventional speed, there is the supersize subsonic jet. The first of these giants was the Boeing 747, which was introduced into airline service by Pan American on January 20, 1970. Generally referred to as a Jumbo Jet, the 747 is almost as long as a football field, nineteen and a half feet in girth, and has a wingspan of over 195 feet. Powered by four mighty Pratt and Whitney turbofan engines, the earliest of the 747s carried up to 450 passengers at speeds of over six hundred miles an hour in greater comfort and for less cost than the SST.

Lockheed followed with its own version of a flying mammoth, the L-1011 Tristar; McDonnell-Douglas with the DC-10; Airbus Industrie of Europe with its A300 series; and then again Boeing with its 757 and 767. All of these high-capacity aircraft are more fuel-efficient and structurally sound than their predecessors. And they are computerized to a degree perhaps not recognized outside the aviation industry. Many of them can virtually fly themselves—or at least be flown without the touch of human hands. This point is underscored by famed aeronautical engineer Willis M. Hawkins, who is senior adviser to the Lockheed Corporation and technical consultant to NASA. As Hawkins notes: "Today one can be transported in comfort from the West Coast of the United States to London (or Paris or Frankfurt) without any of the accompanying crew of the transport ever touching the flying machine. The takeoff, climb, navigation, traffic avoidance, and landing can all be automatic." Hawkins points out that power plants are carefully controlled to minimize fuel consumption. Fuel is pumped from tank to tank to adjust the plane's center of gravity. Flight controls respond immediately to gusts of wind, so that the plane's basic structural loads are not strained. The interior is monitored for constant comfort.

"To get a dramatic picture of what this is all about," Hawkins says, "I recommend that as many as possible try to be invited into the cockpit of a modern transport airplane to see the tools the crew uses. [The technology of] *Star Wars* has been with us for some time."

boom and environmental pollution by exhaust fumes seemed to support their view. Noise and environmental pollution have since been greatly reduced, but the Concorde has not lived up to the airlines' economic expectations. Yet its passengers care less about comfort than about flying across the Atlantic in less than half the time it takes in a subsonic jet. So the Concorde still flies.

Our present subsonic air transports are so successful there's no doubt that they are here to stay. And they will evolve into increasingly advanced forms.

New versions of the jumbo and stretch-length airplanes of the early to mid-1980s will continue to pursue the goal of carrying the greatest numbers of people with peak efficiency. The U.S. Department of Transportation predicts that the next-generation jets are likely to be constructed of lightweight composite materials such as graphite or boron fibers embedded in epoxy. This will reduce the structural weight. The plane's long, slender wings will be swept back and possibly equipped with small winglets at the wingtips to aid forward thrust and save fuel.

Most of the flying will be done by onboard computers, programmed with prearranged flight plans and capable of keeping track of the plane's performance and the operation of its mechanical systems. Complex instrument panels will give way to simplified digital readout screens. Advanced technology turbofan and, later, turboprop engines should increase fuel efficiency by from 12 to almost 30 percent (see Glossary, Turbofan and Turboprop Engines).

The loads these planes can carry will depend on their use. Giant transports may be used as massive passenger craft. (The Federal Aviation Agency projects the probability that a thousand-passenger jumbo jet might be in service by the year 2000.) They may be used as carriers of bulk freight. Or they may be flying ferries, perhaps double-decker planes that accommodate two hundred passengers on the top deck and fifty automobiles in the lower bay.

After that, a natural step will be the supersize transport described in Chapter 1, the Ultra Jet that hovers above an airport as it picks up and delivers passengers and cargo.

At the opposite extreme, we can look for increased use of small passenger aircraft for commuter and corporate travel. Gates Learjet, Cessna, Piper, Beech, and Gulfstream have already introduced new high-performance planes for business use, most of which seat from twelve to twenty passengers in leggy comfort. These new models are

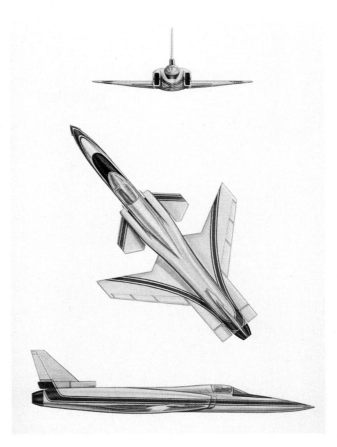

Ring-wing planes such as the one above left, on display at EPCOT Center's World of Motion, would use less fuel than today's planes because they would weigh less; the ring design would reduce the pressure on the wings significantly. Grumman's experimental X-29, above, is a tactical fighter plane featuring a forward swept wing. Reduced drag and weight would mean increased speed and maneuverability, and the cost would be less than today's fighters.

OVERLEAF: In the year 2050, airports will be beehives of carefully orchestrated activity, processing passengers and cargo with equal dispatch. Looming overhead in this artist's conception is a jumbo Ultra Jet—twice the size of a 747, three times faster than an SST—designed to carry people and goods vast distances. The huge plane hovers while it is loaded by flying autoplanes and refueled. Below it on the ground, an enormous twelve-jet cargo plane is being unloaded. At an adjacent heliport (lower left), an airborne cargocopter prepares to land. More freight is delivered from a giant, double-barreled blimp, upper left. Small craft—private supersonic jets and solar-powered planes—taxi down sound-absorbent runways, center. At the perimeter of the airport, short-hop VTOLs (Vertical Takeoff and Landing craft), STOLs (Short Takeoff and Landing craft), and hang gliders (upper right) have special facilities. Computers monitor all of this diverse air traffic with speed and safety.

30 to 50 percent more fuel-efficient, depending on their size, than the older ones still flying. They fly higher and have a greater range—some are transatlantic craft. And they are capable of much better speeds than the present standard of about 300 miles per hour. The Fairchild 400, for example, can fly at more than 400 miles per hour, and the twin-jet Cessna Citation 3 is designed to cruise at 540 miles per hour. There will be more and more of these sleek, high-speed planes that can be used for many purposes, from long-distance business flights to short-haul commuter trips.

But business passengers often need to use small local airports or landing fields with short runways. For this reason, airplanes that can take off and land in limited space are also much in demand and will become increasingly common as corporate craft. One variety is the STOL, or Short Takeoff and Landing airplane, of which the nineteen-passenger de Havilland Twin Otter is an early and popular example. The STOL is designed to lift off the ground without its engine stalling at very low speeds. This means that it can take off from and land on very short runways. Its major drawback is that it is a noisy plane. But several companies in the United States and Europe are working on the development of a quieter STOL-type craft.

A promising though costly variant of the STOL is the VTOL, or Vertical Takeoff and Landing aircraft. The VTOL is similar to a helicopter in that it can rise or set itself down without forward motion. But the typical VTOL has no rotor blades. It is equipped instead with engines that produce upward thrust for takeoff and landing and forward thrust for horizontal flight.

Both STOLs and VTOLs have the potential to offer quick and convenient rides for commuters. Both can use landing fields not much bigger than a parking lot. And both may be useful for airport feeder service or other connecting flights in the one-hundred- to three-hundred-mile range. At present, environmental factors limit their use. But cleaner, quieter, and more efficient STOLs and VTOLs will be built. The FAA considers it likely that a longer, 150-passenger jet STOL will be in operation by the end of the century.

Another likelihood is an improved supersonic airplane. The present Concorde gobbles up three times as much fuel as the jumbo-type subsonic craft. It is also three times as expensive to operate and twice as expensive to build. These costs must be measured against its load capacity, which is one-third that of the 747. It is possible, with today's technology, to build and operate a much larger SST at considerably less than double the cost of a 747—and still maintain the SST's speed advantage.

If we can envision a more practical SST, can a commercial hypersonic craft be far behind? Not very. Major advances in engine power, body structure, and aerodynamic design are all within our technological grasp. Once these advances take place, the possibilities are strong that we can produce a liquid hydrogen—fueled hypersonic transport. It will fly at more than six times the speed of sound at altitudes above a hundred thousand feet.

A slower and lower-flying craft of the near future is the LTA, or Lighter-Than-Air ship. Inspired by blimps and dirigibles, this ultramodern version will not exactly be the Montgolfier balloon or the Zeppelin. It will be a hybrid floater combining helicopter-type power and control systems with the principle of the buoyant hull. The airship's helicopter or STOL-like capability will permit it to take off and land in short distances and at extremely slow speeds. The safe, inert gas in its hull will provide lift at reasonable cost.

An early application of the LTA might well be in passenger transport from outlying areas, such as ranchlands, to regional transportation centers where connections would be made with conventional flights. This would probably be followed by the development of luxury airship services for vacationing travelers. And since the LTA can carry huge and heavy loads at minimal power costs, it will be put to extensive use as a flying crane that can, for example, haul cargo from ship to shore. The LTA could also be used to haul massive cargoes on cross-country flights. It is possible that several giant airships may, in time, replace an entire transcontinental truck fleet.

Controlling Traffic in the Skies

Air traffic of all varieties will multiply so rapidly and become so large that terminal and airfield facilities will necessarily be improved and expanded on a dramatic scale. The possibilities for the future are numerous. Satellite airports will be built to relieve traffic congestion at main airport hubs. Wherever practicable, these may be underground or offshore installations. The trend toward increasing air shipments and small-plane traffic will also produce new facilities. These will include not only major facilities for large passenger-carrying planes, but also special-purpose airports for cargo planes, private planes, and commuter and corporate craft.

To keep up with the enormous volume, the air traffic control system will be upgraded and refined. More personnel may be added. And there will surely be an increased use of computers and various kinds of advanced electronic equipment on planes. This equipment will supply each aircraft with instant readout information on its operation and its flight plan. *Automation* is the word for tomorrow.

In the near future, it is unlikely that the use of petroleum fuels will decline. But as petroleum supplies dwindle, serious consideration will be given to other types of fuel, such as liquid hydrogen, methane, or synthetic jet propellants made from coal. Nuclear power for military aircraft was explored in the 1960s. It was discarded largely because of difficulties in achieving a satisfactory reactor system. But nuclear power may be considered at some future point for civil aircraft if fuel shortages and technical advances make it practical.

Aviation's near future may seem a touch prosaic because of the technological advances we have already put to use. It is easy to become accustomed to automation and computer-controlled operation. But there are still some surprises ahead, and they will be far more innovative than what we now think of as "tomorrow's" systems. Moreover, these surprises may come much faster than we think.

NASA, for instance, is studying new ways of handling the crowded skies with the greatest degree of safety and efficiency. Virtually all options, it appears, depend on greater use of computer-controlled flight operations. This will mean that pilots navigating congested skies and landing at busy airports will be free to monitor all cockpit tasks and use their human brains when human brains are needed.

Scenarios of the future are still in the planning stage. But it seems likely that in the flight deck of tomorrow a short, desk-mounted control stick will take the place of today's bulky steering column. The present complex instrument panels, with their awesome array of dials, flashing lights, and switches, will give way to a bank of perhaps five computer screens that display all the data necessary for flying the plane. The crew will use the onboard computer to program the plane to fly the preselected flight plan. This will trigger the appearance of flight information on the screens. In the course of a flight, the screens display the following:

Screen one—a channel or route in the sky, depicting the aircraft as a blip on a precise path to or from the runway. This screen also presents a navigation map of the selected route and the plan's position on it.

Screen two—information on engines and other systems. Also a landing approach chart and a variety of information about ground conditions.

Screen three—indications that a system is not functioning as it should. Also messages about air traffic.

Screen four—diagrams of various systems and of fuel supply. Also checklists for systems and operation, information now read out by the pilots.

Screen five—another route in the sky and another navigational map, superimposed with weather information for all points en route.

Before it lands, the descending plane receives instructions from the air traffic control computer. From this information, the airplane's computer determines what the airplane's time, speed, and position will be when it makes its final landing approach.

In the coming days of extreme congestion in the skies, planes will have to take off and land even more closely together than in the past. Accuracy will have to be absolute. A system called the Microwave Landing System, or MLS, will provide computerized guidance so precise that planes will be able to make hands-off landings even in cases of zero visibility or when a pilot is incapacitated. An airplane on final approach will enter a channel of microwaves beamed up from the runway. The microwaves will be interpreted by an onboard computer that directs the plane to a pinpoint landing. The practical effect will be to eliminate holding patterns. Planes will be guided down to each runway every forty seconds instead of about every three minutes. Landings will be made with maximum safety even under extremely difficult conditions.

New Plane Designs

Future flights will also benefit from revolutionary changes in the shapes of aircraft. These changes will reduce friction and fuel consumption and, in some cases, increase the plane's load capacity. Several aircraft companies are developing airplanes that will be "flying wings," rather than the winged bodies we now know. Experiments have shown that drag, or air resistance, is greatly reduced when there is little or no fuselage. Lockheed has designed an air freighter that consists almost solely of one 252-foot wing. It is set straight across the top of a comparatively tiny body, and it carries within it the craft's entire payload of some six hundred thousand pounds.

A somewhat different concept is the twin-body or dual-fuselage plane. In this case, two more or less conventional airplane fuselages, or bodies, are attached to the underside of one outsize wing. This design does not reduce drag as much as the pure flying wing. But the payload weight is evenly distributed throughout the craft, so the double shape cuts down on the need for heavy structural support and also reduces fuel consumption. The twin-body may be the answer to economical supersonic flight. It will be able to carry more passengers and consume less fuel than the SSTs of today.

Another design for a supersonic craft, being developed by Rockwell, has a long, lean fuselage. The body, not the wings, provides lift at supersonic speeds. The plane's wing lies flat along the top of the fuselage during cruising flight. The wing pivots outward, returning the plane to a more conventional shape for the slower-speed takeoffs and landings.

A related idea is used in a jet-powered helicopter that has been proposed for the U.S. Navy but could also be used for civil aviation. This plane will have a dual-purpose rotor. It will be put to use in takeoffs and landings. During high-speed flight, it will serve as an X-shaped wing.

Perhaps the oddest-looking of the new designs is the ring-wing aircraft. In this plane, the wings curve upward and over the fuselage and meet at the tips to form a circle. Strange as it looks, the ring-wing is far less subject to stress than conventional wings. Structurally, it is a stronger shape, and it permits the use of lighter construction materials.

Other experts look beyond even these imaginative formulations. They see a hypersonic passenger air carrier of the year 2020 or 2030 that combines the characteristics of a rocket with those of a jet transport. One forecast is for a vehicle that is launched like a rocket into a flight path in space, above the atmosphere. When it reenters the atmosphere, it glides unpowered to an altitude at which its jet engines can be started. The engines then control its descent and permit it to land on a conventional runway like a conventional jet. In this plane, a trip halfway around the world could take forty-five minutes or less—airport to airport.

In another version, the aircraft takes off under conventional turbojet power. At high-altitude cruising speed it switches to scramjet power *(see Glossary, Scramjet)*. It then heads briefly toward space at speeds of well over Mach 6. To complete its journey, it rapidly descends and reverts to normal jet thrust, having added many miles to its route in order to achieve the fastest possible flight.

Hard to believe? McDonnell-Douglas is already at work on a transatmospheric plane that, says a company spokesman, will be able to go anywhere in the world in two hours.

The Pleasure of Flying

In the early days of flying, there were many who took to the skies for the sheer love of flying and who still think nostalgically of the days when the wind is said to have sung in the baling wires. To them, the aircraft of the future may seem like monsters from another world. But that same future promises an exhilarating range of pleasure craft in the sky.

Many of these aircraft will have a basic simplicity. But instead of being novelties, as they are today, in the skies of the future they will be as commonplace as cars now are on our highways. Hang-gliders and other forms of sailplanes, for example, will be highly popular. Small, man-powered aircraft—flying bicycles—along the lines of the pedal-driven *Gossamer Condor* are likely to be as easily used by the general public as road cycles

Powered by a turbofan engine, the WASP is an individual lift device that takes off vertically and flies up to 60 miles per hour. To steer, the rider simply leans in the desired direction.

are today. We'll be seeing more and more personal flyabouts. These will evolve from ultralights, the inexpensive powered gliders of the 1980s. But these flyabouts will be restricted to clearly defined flight paths for the sake of all air traffic. Great colorful balloons, some filled with helium but most sun-powered, will carry vacationers on sightseeing tours over wilderness lands and ancient civilizations. And giant airships will accommodate even more fortunate people on luxury trips around the world.

The best trip of all may be in a derivative of what is now known as the WASP, or Williams Aerial Systems Platform *(see Glossary)*. Built by Williams International of Michigan, the WASP in its present form is a one-man vertical-lift device powered by a small turbofan engine. The pilot stands upright, operating a throttle—maximum speed is about sixty miles per hour—while leaning the craft into the desired direction. Predictably, as the WASP evolves into a vehicle suitable for private ownership, everybody in the world will want one.

At that point, we all will have established our kinship with the Wright brothers and be able to say: "We have done it . . . damned if we ain't flew!"

CHAPTER 7

Giant Steps into Space

Today the early morning sun is bright in the cloudless sky over the Kennedy Space Center in Florida. Looming high above the launchpad is the space shuttle *Challenger,* set for launching at 8:00 A.M. precisely. Supported by its steel cradle, the shuttle is a familiar sight to those who have been following the Space Transportation System program since its first successful flight in April 1981. The shuttle was designed and developed by NASA as the world's first manned, reusable spacecraft. Since its first flight, the shuttle has been subjected to increasingly longer and more complex missions. An ingenious space vehicle, it can carry a 65,000-pound payload into a 240-mile high orbit, and is able to orbit the earth at least one hundred times per trip. On today's flight, the *Challenger* will function primarily as a satellite repair vehicle. Carrying a crew of highly qualified troubleshooters, it will orbit at an altitude of about 190 miles in order to gain access to an unmanned craft in need of repair *(see Glossary, Orbital Flight).* As it travels at 17,500 miles an hour, it will perform a variety of additional tasks and remain aloft for eight days.

On the ground, the shuttle is a massive assemblage consisting of four major components. Towering skyward, dominating the others, is the main fuel tank. This is a huge cylinder measuring 154 feet in length by 27.5 feet in diameter. It contains nearly all the fuel needed to thrust the *Challenger* into orbital flight. The fuel is liquid hydrogen, with a liquid oxygen oxidizer. The tank is the only part of the vehicle that is not recoverable.

Riding piggyback on the tank, also pointing to the sky, is the orbiter, the heart of the system. A fat-bodied rocket plane about the size of a DC-9 passenger aircraft, equipped with three rear-mounted main engines, it is a hardy space truck

---

Repairmen flying small modules service an ailing 21st-century space shuttle (left). The detached passenger cabin (upper right) will dock with another shuttle (lower right) to return to Earth.

Dr. Robert H. Goddard, who launched the first successful liquid-fuel rocket, posed with his historic creation—now in the Smithsonian—in 1926.

that can be used as a workshop and contains living and working quarters for a mission crew of up to seven people. It also contains a sixty-by-fifteen-foot payload bay that can house a space laboratory or transport two or three satellites or a tractor-trailer rig or five elephants. Conventional in some ways, highly unconventional in others, the shuttle is a combination rocket, spaceship, and airplane, a craft that travels variously at hypersonic, supersonic, and subsonic speeds.

Flanking the gigantic main tank filled with liquid propellant are two solid-fuel booster rockets. Each provides an additional 2,650,000 pounds of thrust for blast-off (see Glossary, Thrust). These booster rockets will obtain full thrust power within four-hundredths of a second after ignition and will burn for just two minutes. After that, burnt out, they will be dropped off to be recovered.

The mission crew—commander, pilot, astronauts, and mission specialists—are harnessed into their seats in the orbiter. Checklists are completed.

Seconds pass routinely. The flight will be the same as always—some successes, some disappointments, basically a standard operation that we scarcely even bother to read about anymore.

"Lift-off! We have lift-off!" The digital clock displays 8:00 A.M. to the split second.

Same as always. . . And, as always, the moment of zero countdown, when the twin rockets ignite and the fiery clouds billow beneath the tail of the craft, is a moment of high drama. Mankind is once again soaring into space, where only a few score of us have ever been and only a few thousand will have gone by the end of the century.

But then, the stampede into space will begin.

It is two minutes into the flight. Challenger is twenty-eight miles up. The two booster rockets, their job done, burn out and are dropped off. As they tumble down into the Atlantic, parachutes spring open and balloon out to control their fall. A recovery ship retrieves them for reuse.

Six minutes later, Challenger's three main engines cut off. The huge cylindrical fuel tank, now empty of its liquid propellant, separates from the orbiter and tumbles out to disintegrate in the atmosphere somewhere over the Indian Ocean.

What is left of Challenger now is the chunky swept-back aerospace craft. It is thrust into orbit around the earth by small engines and thrusters. It will maintain its set path until the demands of the mission require maneuvers. When the mission draws to a close, the Challenger's engines and thrusters will maneuver it into position for its entry into the earth's atmosphere.

The Idea of Space Flight

Today's rocketry does not trace its path back directly to the work of any individual or group. Rather it is based on a body of knowledge that has accumulated since the beginning of the twentieth century. The idea of space flight assisted by rockets took shape as a practical possibility in the mind of a Russian teacher and inventor named Konstantin E. Tsiolkovsky. In 1903, Tsiolkovsky published a work called The Investigation of Outer Space by Means of Reaction Apparatus. In this paper he proved, theoretically, that a rocket or "reaction apparatus" could operate in a vacuum.

Travel by rocket in space, which is a vacuum, was therefore possible. A multi-stage liquid fuel rocket, he suggested, might be the most effective means of escaping earth's gravitational pull. The propellants he proposed were hydrogen and oxygen.

Tsiolkovsky died in 1935 and his work was not put to practical use in his time. But his research into rocket propulsion and its uses in interplanetary travel formed a foundation for other scientists to build upon. Unsung except by like-minded investigators, he is today considered the father of the modern science of space travel.

A comparable figure in American rocketry is Robert H. Goddard. He began his speculations on the uses of rockets in space in 1899, when he was 17. In 1926, pursuing his rocket research as a private citizen, he successfully launched the world's first liquid-fuel rocket. Within the next two decades he demonstrated that rockets could be used to carry scientific instruments into the upper atmosphere. In so doing, he paved the way for the manned and unmanned space probes of today.

Goddard's great dream was of space travel between Earth and the moon. He did not live to see it fulfilled. No official agency, in his time, was interested in such space travel. What attracted attention was his pioneering work in practical rocketry, particularly the development of rockets as missiles. Ironically, it was of less interest in the United States than it was to the scientific and military community in Germany.

In the years following World War I, Germany was fertile ground for men of inventive genius. One such man was Hermann Oberth, a Transylvanian who as a youngster had become absorbed with the theory of rockets and the principles of interplanetary travel. By 1930 he was at work in Germany on the development and testing of small liquid-fuel rockets. He soon got help from a young man named Wernher von Braun. Within the next few years, Oberth was overshadowed by von Braun, though the older man continued to contribute significantly to astronautical studies throughout his life. From 1937 to 1945, von Braun was the head of a German research team that successfully developed the V-2 liquid-fuel rocket bomb. This was the first long-range guided

Voyager I, atop a Titan Centaur rocket, blasts off on an interplanetary probe of the far reaches of the solar system in 1977. Below, American astronaut Harrison Schmitt tours the moon's desolate surface on a Lunar Roving Vehicle.

NASA's shuttle flights, begun in 1981, became more complex over the years. In these 1983 photos, Bruce McCandless II (right) models the extravehicular mobility unit (EMU) and the manned maneuvering unit (MMU) that enable crew members to become independent of their spacecraft. On board the orbiting *Challenger*, below, tethered Astronauts F. Story Musgrave and Donald H. Peterson float above the cargo bay. At mission's end, the shuttle, riding on a jet, flies over Houston (above).

missile, and one of the more devastating weapons unleashed against Great Britain in World War II.

But for all its lethal power as a weapon, the V-2 turned out to be far more valuable for its applications to space flight. Its upward speed was more than thirty-five hundred miles per hour. Its range was better than two hundred miles. It reached a height of sixty miles before slowing down and descending. It was, in effect, a space rocket.

At the end of the war, von Braun and more than one hundred other German scientists were brought to the United States to work on additional uses for the wartime flying bomb. Their work, combined with previous American rocket research, led to the development of the type of rockets that would take man to the moon.

Today's space-bound rocket would hold few surprises for such visionaries as Tsiolkovsky and Goddard. Essentially an enormously powerful power plant, it is very similar to a jet engine, except that it does not depend on using oxygen in the atmosphere to oxidize, or burn, its fuel. A rocket carries its own oxidizer. The fuel, typically liquid hydrogen, and the oxidizer, liquid oxygen, together make up the rocket's most vital component, the propellant. The gases produced by the burning of the propellant exit with explosive force from the rear of the rocket. This force provides the thrust that moves the rocket forward.

The United States was not the only nation to realize the potential of the rocket as a tool for explorations beyond the boundaries of Earth. The Russians had also learned from the German V-2 rocket bomb, and it was the Russians who were the first in space. The world's first artificial satellite, *Sputnik I,* was launched by the USSR on October 4, 1957. The second, *Sputnik II,* followed on November 3. Both were hoisted aloft by modified ICBMs, or Intercontinental Ballistic Missiles. They orbited around the earth at about eighteen thousand miles per hour. Small though they were, and unmanned, they were the greatest breakthrough in transportation since the first flight of the Wright brothers' airplane.

To see their tiny distant glint in the night sky was to catch a glimpse of the beginning of a new era in the life of Earth's people.

Explorer I, a tiny capsule that was the first American space satellite, soared into orbit on January 31, 1958.

With its launch, a race of sorts began.

In 1959, the USSR landed an unmanned rocket on the moon. In hot pursuit, the United States speeded up its Mercury program of suborbital flight. But on April 12, 1961 the Soviet Union achieved another major first by putting a manned spacecraft in orbit. This was *Vostok I,* crewed by cosmonaut Yuri Gagarin.

Later that year, two Americans—first, Alan B. Shepard, Jr., then Virgil I. "Gus" Grissom—separately made two brief suborbital flights. These were almost immediately overshadowed by a Russian orbital flight of more than twenty-five hours.

The next man in space was Lieutenant Colonel John Glenn. On February 20, 1962, riding the Mercury capsule *Friendship 7,* Glenn became the first American to orbit the earth.

By that time, President John F. Kennedy had committed the United States to the goal of a landing on the moon by the end of the 1960s. An enormous technological and scientific program to reach that goal was already under way.

The first indication that success was near came on December 21, 1968. Astronauts Frank Borman, James A. Lovell, Jr., and William Anders traveled a quarter of a million miles into space in the Apollo spacecraft, which was powered by a Saturn rocket. For nearly 20 hours of the 147 hours of their mission, they circled the moon, sending televised views of the lunar surface back down to earth and obtaining information that would be invaluable for the first landing.

That came on July 20, 1969, when American spacemen Neil A. Armstrong and Edwin E. "Buzz" Aldrin, Jr. walked, half floating, on the moon's dusty surface. They were the first human beings to set foot on any celestial body other than the earth.

Five more lunar landings followed in the course of the next three and a half years. The final landing came on the Apollo 17 mission of December 1972, when astronauts Eugene A. Cernan and Harrison H. Schmitt stayed on the moon for a record seventy-five hours.

Meanwhile, the USSR had successfully placed a Salyut space laboratory into long-term orbit.

As the Apollo program was drawing to a close, the United States began a new American phase of space exploration and study with its manned experimental workshop, called Skylab.

Launched in May 1973, Skylab was an earth-orbiting space station that served as a laboratory and living quarters for three astronauts at a time. The main capsule was a redesigned and modified third stage of a Saturn V moon rocket. It was sent unmanned into earth orbit. Later, each of three successive three-man teams of astronaut-scientists was launched from earth in a modified Apollo spacecraft that docked with the Skylab station in orbit.

The Shuttle Takes Form

These commuter-type trips of the astronaut-scientists led to the development of a shuttle system that would use reusable components. The con-

cept centered on a spacecraft that could be launched into orbit with its crew to perform a series of tasks and return to earth to land on a runway like an airplane. It could then be overhauled for an indefinite number of future missions.

Thus was born the space shuttle, a maneuverable rocket ship that can repeatedly travel from earth to orbit and back. The first one, the *Columbia,* made its round-trip maiden voyage in April 1981, and returned five times to space. *Columbia* was joined by *Challenger,* another successful repeater which began its series of flights in April 1983. So began a long series of shuttle missions.

At first, the shuttles served primarily as orbiting laboratories, carrying the test station Spacelab, which was developed by the European Space

In this artist's conception, a Space Shuttle Orbiter, upper left, approaches a working, permanently manned, modularized space station in Earth orbit.

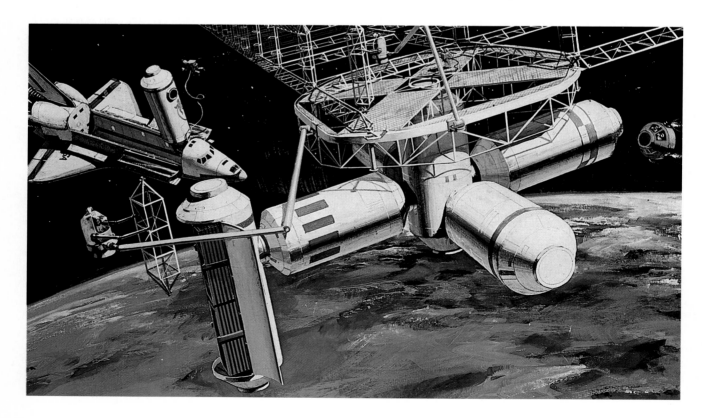

Shown under construction, Spacelab, a joint NASA/European Space Agency venture, was designed as an orbital laboratory to be carried in the shuttles' bays.

Agency. But they have since developed into remarkably versatile vehicles. At any one time a shuttle might be a carrier of personnel, cargo, and laboratory equipment. It might be a test station for a variety of experiments. Or it might be a launching base for satellites and even jet-powered astronauts. The shuttle is manned and highly maneuverable. This means that it is capable of meeting up with other objects in orbit and then serving as a maintenance shop. Space repairmen could jet out from it to repair malfunctioning telescopes, observatories, or other satellites. If necessary, a shuttle might even retrieve a satellite and carry it to earth in its payload bay for a major overhaul. Then again, a shuttle might be a survey ship probing the globe for potential resources. It might be a plant for the manufacture of exotic materials. Or it might be a rocketing space truck delivering materials for the construction of space stations, while serving as a base for the builders of those stations.

Every year, the number of flights is scheduled to increase: ten in 1984, twelve in 1985, seventeen in 1986, twenty-four in 1987. So it will go, until, by the year 2000, there will have been between five and six hundred shuttle flights. Ultimately, the *Columbias* and the *Challengers* and the orbiters following them will be an accepted, everyday part of our culture, as common a part of our lives as the automobile in the 1920s and the airplane two decades later.

Moving Out Into Space

America's Skylab, Russia's Salyut, and even the orbital missions of the shuttles can be regarded as trial runs for the true space stations presently being planned by the National Aeronautics and Space Administration. The current challenge, according to NASA, is to decide what specific approach makes the most sense and can be done for the least cost. (Whatever the approach, the cost is expected to reach $8 billion.) Predictions are that the initial components of our first space station can be assembled in earth orbit by 1992—or perhaps, according to more optimistic NASA spokesmen, by 1990. Important considerations are the size of the space station and the quality of life for those who will be occupying it for extended periods of time.

Various different designs have already been considered. But at present the basic concept calls for a station assembled out of several elements, each of which would be hauled aloft separately in the cargo bay of a shuttle. The units would then be clustered together by astronaut-workers to form a habitable space station. This spacehab will be small at first, consisting of four or five pressurized units linked together like pieces of a three-dimensional jigsaw puzzle or an adult erector set. Part of the station will serve as living and working quarters for crews of six to eight people. Another section will house the power, environmental control, and data processing operations for the entire unit. And probably one unit will be equipped as a dock for space shuttles. In this way, the space station would receive regular deliveries of food and supplies, additional building materials, and, periodically, replacement personnel.

It is expected that the station will be continuously occupied, with crews rotating every three to six months. After perhaps two or three years of the station's life, the resident population for any duty tour might be increased to twelve or possibly even twenty individuals. New units would be added to accommodate them.

Crews will live in an earthlike atmosphere, breathing as if at sea level. Yet they will be able to move about effortlessly in the weightlessness of space. Their quarters will be compact but adequately equipped with sleeping cubicles, exercise areas, dining quarters, bathroom facilities—all the necessities of life, and more comforts than America's westward pioneers ever knew.

Yet the little outpost will be devoted to an ambitious work program. Extending from the central core of the station will be solar-powered wings and booms holding a variety of sensitive monitoring instruments. Unmanned modules, either attached to the station or orbiting nearby, will carry self-contained equipment for additional scientific observations and for manufacturing certain crystals, drugs, and new types of food. Almost from its inaugural, the space station will be a national and perhaps even international facility. It will be available for use by scientific groups and private industry for any number of ventures.

The space station will, in fact, serve numerous purposes, which will increase as time goes by. Even more than Skylab or the Spacelab missions of 1983, it will be a factory as well as a laboratory, a test habitation as well as a vehicle, and a total experiment in space life—complete with trips outdoors. In its role as a practical workshop, the station and its crew will be able to service satellites and build other space stations without feeling the press of time. Repair and construction personnel will be aided in their work by two vehicles—the MMU, or manned maneuvering unit, and the unmanned space tug *(see Glossary, MMU and Space Tug)*.

The MMU is the famous "Buck Rogers" propulsion backpack designed for one-man operation. It was first tested during the *Challenger* shuttle mission of February 1984. Looking something like an overstuffed armchair without a seat, this device contains two refillable fuel cylinders of nitrogen gas, twenty-four tiny jet thrusters, and an electronic control system. Extending from the main body of the backpack are two armrests with built-in, hand-operated maneuvering controls at their ends. The jet-powered astronaut is strapped into this flying contraption and breathes oxygen from a small life-support backpack. He or she can then orbit along with the space station at eighteen thousand miles per hour, using the controls to steer to the work site and stay in position while working.

The space tug, or unmanned orbital maneuvering vehicle, is presently under development. It will supplement both the shuttle and the space station. Delivered to orbit by shuttle and commanded by signals from the ground, the tug will be able to maneuver orbiting objects from one orbit to another. It will be able to boost aging satellites back into place when their orbits begin to droop.

Tugs promise to be highly useful workhorses in space. They could retrieve and deliver payloads to altitudes far beyond the reach of the massive shuttle. They could put satellites in position and bring them back to the space station for servicing. And they could be used to haul material and move objects around when workers built new structures in space—including auxiliary space stations.

Eventually, according to NASA, our flagship space station could serve two other purposes. It could be a staging area for planetary probes. And it could be a supply depot for traffic to bases on the moon and even Mars. It will be, says Jesco von Puttkamer, a senior NASA program planner, "a transportation hub—a little Cape Canaveral in orbit."

Communities in the Sky

Meanwhile, is there any possibility of a Moon Base Alpha, a first base on the moon, within the lifetime of those who witnessed, through blurry television pictures, man's first steps on the moon? NASA says there is, especially if we were youngsters at the time. NASA's hope is to return to the moon and establish a base there by the year 2008. Will there be a permanent civilian settlement? Probably not.

Those whose contracts oblige them to live on the moon for certain periods to mine its valuable minerals will almost certainly be housed underground. That will protect them from the bitter cold and merciless darkness of the fourteen-day lunar

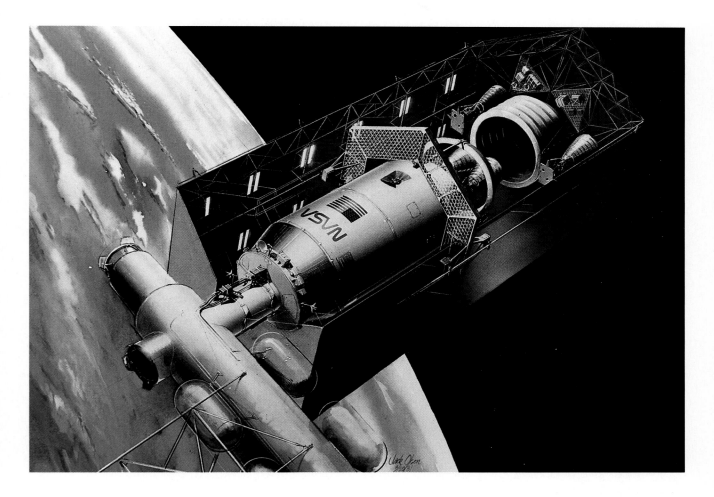

Berthed in the hangar of an orbiting Space Operations Center, a space-based reusable Orbital Transfer Vehicle undergoes servicing between flights.

night and the heat and searing brightness of the equally long lunar day. There will be space factories and industrial sites and residential quarters as comfortable as they can be made. But long-term residents in these first decades of space settlement are far more likely to be living in artificial colonies located at a point roughly equidistant between the earth and the moon.

That point in space is also the most likely location for the establishment of communities in space, according to Gerard K. O'Neill, physicist at

the Space Studies Institute of Princeton University. The space settlers in these communities, O'Neill points out, will be exploiting the new frontier for their own reasons as individuals and also for the benefit of all humanity. The high frontier, O'Neill says, "is a frontier of new lands, located only a few days' travel time away from the earth, and built from materials and energy available in space." The energy comes from the sun, the materials from the moon.

In O'Neill's view, large-scale space industries should be well under way before the turn of the century. They will both demand and invite the presence of hundreds and even thousands of people who will live in high orbit for long periods of time. Thus the first space colonies will also be in existence by the year 2000. The size and design of these colonies will change in the course of time. But the first space colony, says O'Neill, will be in the shape of a wheel or a torus, a doughnut-shaped structure. This structure will spin slowly to provide a simulation of Earth's gravity for its residents, and it will contain an atmosphere with the same oxygen content as that of sea-level Earth. Inhabitants will grow all their own food and get all the energy they need from the sun.

The colony envisioned by the Princeton futurist will house ten thousand people. Almost all of them will be occupied with building additional islands in space for subsequent generations of colonists. "By the middle years of the next century," O'Neill says, "the first beachhead in space will have grown to include thousands of such colonies, each with a language and a cultural heritage drawn from a nation of earth. Travel between earth and its colonies will be as common by then as international travel is today."

Von Puttkamer adds: "Beyond the year 2000, tourism will develop as the biggest, most lucrative, and most dynamic commercial interest—bigger than industry and research. And within one hundred years, space will be teeming with tourists seeking the ultimate experience—a sense of high adventure and deep spiritual satisfaction.".

Journey to a Space Colony

It is some time during the last quarter of the twenty-first century, and we are among a group of travelers that includes some vacationers and many new workers at various islands in the sky. We are embarking on the greatest experience of our lives as we check in at the departure building of International Space City, the new Earth Interna-

In low Earth orbit near a space station is a lunar ferry (center). It has a rigid aerobraking shield to reduce speed upon re-entry and carries fuel tanks at front and rear. A propellant dump is at lower left.

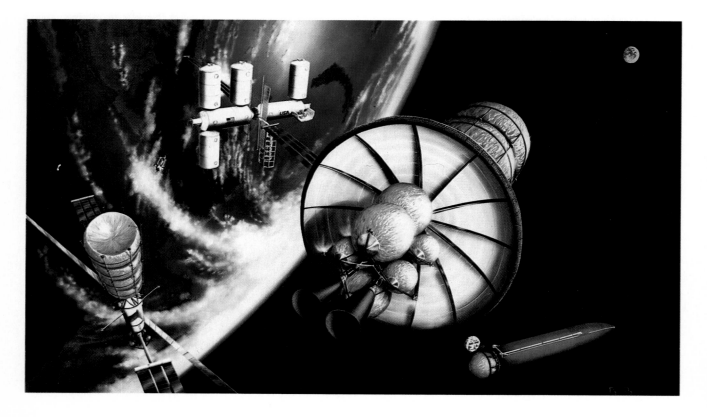

tional Space Port. After checking in, we are taken by automated minitrain to the launch area for the passenger shuttle. The craft is not unlike the shuttling space trucks of the turn of the century. But its rocketry is infinitely more advanced.

Our destination is a distant space colony called Armstrong II. Other passengers will be heading for other space colonies, orbital factories, bases on the moon, and settlements farther out in space.

Blast off is as much a thrill as ever—but after that, it is a brief and routine trip to the low-orbit pioneer colony that is now the primary way station in space. This early construction, called America I, looks very much like a gigantic floating doughnut, but it spins like a slow-moving top. Its indoor world houses more than ten thousand permanent occupants and a transient population of several hundred. The curved interior is earthlike and has simulated blue skies and clouds, real green plants, animals, birds in the trees, sparkling streams, hills, valleys, lakes, and attractive housing whose residents look out over fields and forests. Gravity is earth-normal in the residential areas, but much reduced near the hub of the structure, where the space port is located.

We dock and are whisked to a space hotel where we will await the arrival of a deep-space vehicle. This enormous cruiser, an oddly shaped craft of many modules and compartments, will take various groups of space travelers to the vicinity of other stations, planets, or moons. Serviced by other craft as it goes on its perpetual journey between space ports, the vast space liner never lands. We'll be rocketed out to it by local shuttle.

Next morning—or what passes for morning in our artificial environment—the great ship is hovering overhead. The shuttle takes us to it in minutes. We dock, and attendants show us to our quarters. Boosted by small thrusters, the cruiser lifts out of orbit into deeper space.

Our craft pauses over the moon, and an awkward-looking little moon-lander links up with us to exchange passengers. None of the vehicles out here in space is streamlined or looks in any way like an airplane. Since there is no air resistance, the various spaceships are built in any shape that suits their practical purpose.

A solar sail craft, propelled by photons from the sun reflecting off its miles of aluminized sheeting, meets Halley's Comet in the painting above.

We go on, every once in a while hovering in the vicinity of other communities to exchange other groups of passengers. Finally, we ourselves are shuttled from the spacecruiser to the sky island. Here we will live and work in earthlike surroundings for the next two years, spending our vacations with friends on other sky islands.

Reaching Out to Distant Stars

Looking farther ahead into a future difficult for us to imagine, much less comprehend, we might at some very distant day watch the takeoff of a Space Ark. This spaceship will head for the stars of another solar system that is so far away we cannot express the distance in miles or millions of miles but only in light years. A light year is the distance light travels in one year: 5,876,000,000,000,000—almost six trillion—miles. Alpha Centauri, the star nearest our solar system—but not necessarily one with habitable planets—is about 4.3 light years away.

If the Space Ark is anything like the USS *Enterprise* of the frequently re-run television show "Star Trek," it will cruise easily at the speed of light and be able to reach much greater velocities. At our present level of knowledge, we know of nothing in the universe that can travel faster than the speed of light, which is 186,000 miles per second. It is not surprising that it has become an accepted law of nature that nothing *can.* Even getting near that speed, it is believed, will require enormous amounts of energy in some form as yet undiscovered and untamed. The producers of "Star Trek" were faced with the problem of powering the fictional *Enterprise* on its unimaginably long space voyage.

To achieve these distances, the starship would need to travel at incredible speeds. As the source of power, the producers chose antimatter—difficult to make, extremely difficult to handle, virtually impossible to contain, but pure energy. The choice was a happy one. The *Enterprise* zipped from planet to planet at speeds as fast and faster than the speed of light. These speeds were measured in "warp factors." Warp Factor One was the speed of light, a mere stroll in the country. Warp Factor Three was twenty-four times that speed. And Warp Factor Six, used when the action became earnest, was *216* times the speed of light.

Unbelievable! Yet scientists seriously believe the use of antimatter as a fuel is a possibility that may hold great promise for the future of space travel. The Ark of the distant future may actually be a kind of *Enterprise II.*

If this does not come to pass, the alternative might well be a lumbering frontier wagon of a ship powered by something like a fusion ramjet *(see Glossary, Ramjet)*. This nuclear engine is yet to be developed. Technologically, it is far more accessible and efficient than the antimatter power of the *Enterprise,* even if incapable of the latter's faster-than-the-speed-of-light pace.

Preprogrammed and completely automated, this star voyager might embark upon a silent odyssey that would last perhaps twenty-five thousand years, perhaps fifty thousand, perhaps more. It might take its varied cargo to an outer world preselected as a new home base for mankind—a replacement for old Spaceship Earth. Or it might be heading for a planetary outpost from which deep-space explorations might eventually be launched.

In addition to construction equipment, robots, and all manner of start-up materials, the craft would be likely to carry a complete stock of animals, people, and plants. They would not be fully animated or even grown but in the form of frozen embryos, seeds, and spores. In this manner, the incredible journey could take place without any living thing being conscious of its passage.

Finally, on arrival at the destination planet, computer-activated robots would set to work revitalizing the suspended life forms.

The prospect of such a voyage is not one that need be considered for a good many hundreds or thousands of years. We still have to reach and humanize the stepping stones in space.

This is no small challenge. But it is surely within our scope. If there is a place to go on the high frontier, we will find a way to get to it and a way to make it livable. *Transportation* is the key to our future in space. Transportation is the ability to get to wherever we want to go. Transportation is essential to progress, to moving on and increasing our complexity as human beings. The technology of transportation is going to take us deep into space, no matter what the difficulties.

And this is not a dream of a far-off future.

"The human race stands now on the threshold of a new frontier whose richness is a thousand times greater than that of the new Western world of 500 years ago," says Princeton's Gerard O'Neill. "By 2150," O'Neill maintains, "there could be more people living in space than on earth.... Earth might serve mainly as a tourist attraction—a carefully preserved monument to man's origin."

Better yet, far from becoming a monument, Earth will endure as a vital, growing planet whose progress includes the taming of its new frontier in space. Then the billions of us living on Earth will be able to look up into the night sky and see the pinpoints and clusters of light that man himself has arranged in space—just a few thousand years after that clever Sumerian invented the wheel.

Countless eons from now, man may embark on an epic voyage aboard an interstellar ark in an effort to perpetuate earthly life somewhere out in space.

Glossary

Aerodynamics The study of the effect of the flow of air and other gases on moving objects. Aerodynamics is based on the study of motion.

APT (Advanced Passenger Train) A train that travels at high speeds on curving tracks. As the cars go around a curve, they tilt on their bogies, or wheel units.

Autoplane Still in the planning stage, an autoplane is a combination airplane and car. On landing, the wings of the vehicle fold back so it can be driven on a highway.

Bullet Train A high-speed train developed in Japan. The Bullet Train runs on a specially built track.

Fuel Cell A fuel cell produces electricity without flame or pollution by means of a chemical reaction.

Hovercraft A vehicle that travels by moving above the surface of water or land on a cushion of air created by fans and propellers.

Hydrofoil A boat that skims along the surface of the water, riding on ski-like runners also called hydrofoils.

Hypersonic Transport Planes Not yet developed, hypersonic transport planes would be able to fly above 100,000 feet at a speed of Mach 5, using liquid hydrogen as a fuel (see Supersonic Speed).

Internal Combustion Engine An internal combustion engine burns fuel in a chamber inside the engine. The fuel is ignited by a spark or, in a diesel engine, by hot compressed air. The explosion of the fuel creates an expanding gas that moves a piston, which produces work, such as turning a car's wheels.

Mach Number Mach numbers are used to indicate the speed of aircraft in comparison with the speed of sound. A plane flying at the speed of sound, 660 miles per hour at altitudes above sea level, is said to be flying at a speed of Mach 1.

Maglev (Magnetically Levitated Train) A high-speed train that floats inches above the track on a cushion of air created by powerful electromagnets.

MMU (Manned Maneuvering Unit) A one-man propulsion device used by astronauts to leave a spacecraft and maneuver in space.

Monorail A monorail is a vehicle, usually above street level, that rides on one rail.

Orbital Flight Orbital flight is the circular flight in space around the earth or another celestial body.

PeopleMover PeopleMovers are a form of short-distance transportation using a moving walkway or one or more cars.

Planetran (Rocket Train) A rocket-powered train of the future that would travel underground.

Ramjet A high-speed engine with no turbine, compressor, or other moving parts. Air that is sucked into a ramjet engine is compressed because of the great speed at which it enters the engine (see Scramjet).

Resistance Air resists, or holds back, the movement of a plane or car moving through it. Water resists, or holds back, the movement of a boat.

Rocket Engine A rocket engine burns liquid or solid fuel, which becomes a gas and expands. The expanding gas, rushing out of the rocket's exhaust, creates a force called thrust (see Thrust).

Scramjet (Supersonic Combustion Ramjet) An experimental engine for planes that would fly at very high altitudes at speeds of Mach 12 to 15. This engine could burn air and liquid oxygen in a supersonic combustion chamber (see Ramjet).

Space Tug An unmanned vehicle currently under development by NASA. Carried into space by the shuttle, it would be controlled from the ground and used by astronauts to do work in space.

STOL (Short Takeoff and Landing Plane) An aircraft with special engines that permit it to take off and land on a very short runway at low speeds without stalling.

Supersonic Speed Speed that is faster than the speed of sound. Supersonic speeds range from Mach 1 to Mach 5; speeds above Mach 5 are called hypersonic (see Mach Number).

Thrust Thrust is the force that moves an airplane or rocket forward. In a jet or rocket engine, thrust is produced by the force created when powerful hot gases escape from the rear of the engine. In a propeller-driven plane, thrust is provided by the propeller.

Turbine Engine A turbine engine is a rotary engine powered by the force of water, steam, or hot gases. It has a series of blades mounted on a central rotating wheel. The force of the liquid or gas striking against the blades makes the wheel turn which provides the power to do work.

Turbofan Engine A turbofan, or bypass, engine is an adaptation of the turbojet engine. It has a special fan that sends air back to the engine's exhaust. This cool air improves engine efficiency and reduces noise.

Turbojet Engine (Jet Engine) In a turbojet or jet engine, air is sucked into the engine by fans called compressors. The air goes into a combustion chamber where it combines with fuel and burns, producing expanding gases (see Thrust).

Turboprop Engine In a turboprop engine, as in a turbojet engine, escaping gases provide thrust to move the plane. But the turboprop engine also has additional turbines that turn a standard propeller.

Ultra Jet A double-decker plane of the future which loads passengers and cargo while hovering in the air.

VTOL (Vertical Takeoff and Landing Plane) VTOL aircraft take off and land by moving straight up and down. They can also fly horizontally like standard airplanes.

WASP (Williams Aerial Systems Platform) The WASP is a one-person flying device that is powered by a small turbofan engine.

Index

Boldface numbers indicate illustrations.